**W9-CRZ-877**

# Guiding Light

## Centered in Christ
## CYCLE C

Homilies by Fr. Joe Robinson

Shepherds of Christ Publications
P.O. Box 627
China, Indiana 47250 USA

Toll free USA: (888) 211-3041
Tel: (812) 273-8405
Fax: (812) 273-3182
Email: info@sofc.org
http://www.sofc.org

Second Printing: 2013

In honor

of our

Beloved Priests

We want Adoration Chapels
around the world –
The Mighty Medicine

# Foreward

Dear Father,

I give my heart to Jesus and Mary with you in love.

In the world today it is good for us to remember, what our founder, Fr. Carter said, the individual Christian, the Church and the world is in the state of becoming.

## Priestly Writing and Prayers

In 18 years of this Movement we have sent loose and in books, over 17,000,000 Priestly Newsletters to priests and hierarchy. We have prayer chapters praying for the priests, the Church and the world all over the world (found in the backs of this book and most of our books), on a page brochure we enclosed in previous mailings. This is a network of prayer in 8 languages around the world. We believe these prayer chapters, many 18 years old, can be a network of prayer praying for the priests, the Church and the world, giving great devotion to the Sacred Heart and Immaculate Heart, now, and in the future when we are gone.

We pray 24 hours a day before the exposed Eucharist in China, Indiana for you and all your work in helping the Church to be what God wants it to be in all its members. (picture enclosed on rear inside cover) We love the Church, the pillar of truth, and we give our lives living, in recognition of this calling, to pray for the Church and the world and for all our priests and to circulate these writings on the spiritual life.

## The Word

It is exciting to me, Rita Ring, co-founder of Shepherds of Christ, to read Fr. Joe's homilies (my brother) and my love of the Word grows ever more and more. We want the Word to live in us. It is a two-edged sword. The Word in our hearts aiding us in making our contribution in helping to build the Kingdom using the unique God-given talents God gave us.

## The Father's Family

God is our Creator, we were created uniquely with a purpose to make our unique contribution to the building of the Father's family. Living in love as brothers and sisters and realizing we are to contribute in helping to make the Church and the world more as God intends.

## Our Christ Life and Our Mission

In the sacrament of baptism, we receive a sharing in His life. We are to grow in this Christ-life making the contribution God wants as we live more deeply in Him.

We sing the song *Seek Ye First the Kingdom of God*.

I wrote the song *Glory, Glory, Glory Lord* and *A Priest is a Gift from God*.

We are so thankful for all you do.

We are so thankful for all our priests.

Fr. Carter, S. J. Doctorate, founder of the Shepherds of Christ, believed he was called by God in this mission to send the Priestly Writings. Fr. Carter said Jesus told him to pray these particular prayers and begin these prayer chapters around the world, praying for the priests, the Church and the world. We have begun these prayer chapters for over 18 years now since 1994.

## The Mass

We as members of the mystical body of Christ can help in being united to the Mass with pure hearts – all day – offering up our every day works, serving God according to His will in love. It is in the interior offering in our hearts that we want to be pure, holy, loving and following in Jesus' footsteps – in all we do – united to the Masses going on around the world – praying for grace to be outpoured for our priests, the Church and the world.

God is love and we are to pray in love for our brothers and sisters of the world, relying on God's Might.

The Mass is the sacrifice of Calvary sacramentally made present – a fountain of grace being poured out on us hungry, hungry souls. We adore God, we thank God, we petition God for grace for the Church and the world and we want to help make reparation for our sins and the sins of the world.

## Consecration to the Hearts of Jesus and Mary

We give ourselves in Consecration to the Hearts of Jesus and Mary and we pray to God to help us grow in our graced life until we are with Him wrapped in His embrace for all eternity.

Please help us spread these prayer chapters praying for the priests, the Church and the world and giving great devotion to the Pure and Holy Hearts of Love of Jesus and Mary.

## The Father's Plan – Love

I heard a song once, it said "What the world needs now is love." The Plan of the Father is that we love God with our whole heart, our whole soul and our whole being and that we love our neighbor as ourselves.

God is love. God first loved us. It is our response to God's love.

Man is made in the image and likeness of God, so we are to love!

Happiness is found in God.

Spread the Good News, Jesus has died, He has risen and this is our call in this life – to love – to pray for the priests, the Church and the world.

## Homilies from Fr. Joe, My Brother

I, with all of us at Shepherds of Christ, pray that you, God's holy chosen one, will be blessed. This sixth book of homilies from Fr. Joe Robinson, my brother, is a cherished gift he has allowed us to send to you.

Sincerely and with much love in the Hearts of Jesus and Mary,

Rita Robinson Ring, Co-founder
Shepherds of Christ Ministries

John Weickert, our President, has given much to make this happen and all our faithful people, Servants and Handmaids of the Good Shepherd and Apostles of the Eucharistic Heart of Jesus and Associates of the Sacred Heart of Jesus.

# Prayer Before the
# Holy Sacrifice of the Mass

Let me be a holy sacrifice and unite with God in the sacrament of His greatest love.

I want to be one in Him in this act of love, where He gives Himself to me and I give myself as a sacrifice to Him. Let me be a holy sacrifice as I become one with Him in this my act of greatest love to Him.

Let me unite with Him more, that I may more deeply love Him. May I help make reparation to His adorable Heart and the heart of His Mother, Mary. With greatest love, I offer myself to You and pray that You will accept my sacrifice of greatest love. I give myself to You and unite in Your gift of Yourself to me. Come and possess my soul.

Cleanse me, strengthen me, heal me. Dear Holy Spirit act in the heart of Mary to make me more and more like Jesus.

Father, I offer this my sacrifice, myself united to Jesus in the Holy Spirit to You. Help me to love God more deeply in this act of my greatest love.

Give me the grace to grow in my knowledge, love and service of You and for this to be my greatest participation in the Mass. Give me the greatest graces to love You so deeply in this Mass, You who are so worthy of my love.

*by* Rita Robinson Ring
*Imprimatur:* Archdiocese of Cincinnati.

# Table of Contents
## Cycle C – 2012 / 2013

**Certificate of Marriage**

I, the undersigned, do hereby certify, that on the 25 day of June A.D. 19 36
in the church of St. Boniface I joined in the

**Holy Bonds of Matrimony**

William M. Robinson and Alice Weber

according to the rites of the Holy Roman Catholic Church.

Henry J. Robinson

Witness: Marie Weber

Rev. John H. Schwartz
Pastor

Dedicated to William and Alice Robinson.

Our Mother and Father married on
June 25, 1936 in St. Boniface Church, Cincinnati.

# 1st Sunday of Advent
## November 29, 2009

**INTRODUCTION** – (Jeremiah 33:14-16; 1 Thess. 3:12-4:2; Luke 21:25-28,34-36) The prophet, Jeremiah, lived during one of the most devastating times in the history of Israel. He witnessed the Babylonian invasion which brought with it the destruction of the city of Jerusalem along with its Temple, the only Temple of the Jewish people. He saw many of his fellow citizens enslaved and taken into exile. Yet his words reflect hope and not despair. His hope is based not on human capabilities but on God's faithfulness to God's promises. Jeremiah recalls God's promise to his people made over 400 years earlier – during the time of King David. God would bring to the throne a successor to the King who would bring peace and security to Jerusalem. We still wait for peace and security – not only in Jerusalem but all over the world. The promised one, a descendant of the House of David, has begun his reign. The gospel tells us one day he will come in great glory to complete his work and to establish the kingdom of God forever.

**HOMILY** – You may have heard this one before. It's about a fellow who wanted a Lexus for Christmas. So a few weeks before Christmas he went to his parish priest and asked: "Would you do a novena for me so I get a Lexus for Christmas?" The priest said, "I need to ask one question first: 'What's a Lexus?'" So the fellow thought it was probably a lost cause. I'll ask someone else. So he went to a nearby Church where a Franciscan priest was a pastor and he asked him: "Would you do a novena for me so I get a Lexus for Christmas?" The poor, humble priest said, "I need to ask one question: 'What's a Lexus?'" The fellow thought, "I won't get anywhere here." So he went to the local Jesuit parish and asked the pastor: "Would you do a novena for me so I get a Lexus for Christmas?" The Jesuit priest said, "I have one question I need to ask, 'What's a novena?'"

Never let it be said that you came to St. Boniface and never heard the word "novena." It comes from the Latin word "novem." That's how November got its name because originally in the Roman calendar November was the ninth month of the year. A novena is nine days of prayer or sacrifice for a special intention or to prepare for a special feast. Many people make a novena of prayer for the gift of the Holy Spirit right before Pentecost. Today starts Advent, a time to prepare for the celebration of the birth of Jesus. Advent is longer than nine days – this year it's more like three novenas, 27 days. We might consider including the spirit of novena, prayer and sacrifice, as part of our Christmas preparations. Buying gifts, decorating, sending cards and going to parties might be nice but how much do they do for our inner self, our spirit, besides maybe wear us out? Jesus tells us pointedly in today's gospel, "Be careful not to let your hearts be weighed down from dissipation and drunkenness and the anxieties of this life ... but be alert at all times and pray..." In the midst of all our preparations for Christmas, we have to work at making this also a time of spiritual preparation or Christ's birth will be a shallow event for us. If his birth is an event without much depth of spiritual meaning for us, neither will any other part of our faith have much depth of meaning, including the beautiful gift of himself he gives us in the Eucharist.

Jesus' first coming was simple and humble, his coming to us now in the poor, in prayer and sacrament is experienced mostly by faith, but his coming in the future will be glorious and unmistakable, although it will be frightful for some as he tells us in today's gospel. On this first Sunday of Advent, we prepare for his coming by beginning to tell his story again: the story of his birth, his miracles and teaching, his death and resurrection. St. Luke will be our mentor through much of this year. When I taught religion in high school, I would often introduce a topic and the students would complain: "We studied that in grade school." The implication being, of course, that they thought they knew all there was to know about the topic. We might be tempted to think the same thing as we begin again to tell Jesus' story: "we heard that last year." But we're not the same person we were last year, or the year before. We've grown older, we've encountered new experiences, we may have made new friends or other friends have gone out of our lives, we most likely see things a little differently than we did a year or two ago. As we hear it again, we will see the story of Jesus perhaps a little differently than we did a year ago, perhaps it will mean a little more to us than it did then. Although the story of Jesus does not change, we do. We have to keep hearing it over and over to fully appreciate it for it is a story of infinite love, a story of infinite meaning that will continue to speak to us. We will never exhaust the richness of the love Christ has shown us. Amen.

## 2nd Sunday of Advent
### December 6, 2009

**INTRODUCTION** – (Baruch 5:1-9; Philippians 1:3-6,8-11; Luke 3:1-6) In today's first reading, we hear from Baruch, the secretary of Jeremiah the prophet. He lived during the Babylonian exile over 500 years before Christ. When the Babylonians conquered Jerusalem, they destroyed everything and took most of its citizens to Babylon as captives. Our first reading has as its background this experience of the exile. Baruch speaks to the demolished city of Jerusalem and tells it to rejoice, for it will prosper again. If they look east (toward Babylon) they will see God gathering his people together to bring them back home. It is indeed a message of hope. Another prophet, Isaiah, also wrote about this return of God's people from exile and we hear that passage quoted in today's gospel.

**HOMILY** – I want to start with a brief history lesson which many of you may know already, but it won't hurt to hear it again. The Babylonian exile took place 587 years before Christ. Many Jews were killed, of course, when the Babylonians conquered Jerusalem. Those Jews who lived through the invasion of the Babylonians were enslaved and transported to Babylon. Babylon was located in modern day Iraq, less than 100 miles south of Baghdad. For 700 years the Jews had lived in their own land and for almost 440 years they had their own king. God spoke through his prophets that this exile was not to last, but that he would bring his people home again. And so we heard Baruch and Isaiah speak words of hope to God's people at this difficult time. The prophets encouraged them to continue believing and trusting in God. Not quite 50 years later, Babylon was conquered by the Persians (which is modern day Iran). The king of Persia (Cyrus) gave permission for the Jews to return to their homeland. You have seen enough news' programs, I'm sure, to know what the terrain is like in that area. There were ancient roads along the rivers but there was also lots of wilderness and mountains and deserts. We must remember the promise of return is in poetic form, thus the prophets tell the people God would bring them back on royal thrones, the mountains would be made low, the rugged ways would be smoothed out, the valleys would be filled in and everyone would know God was saving his people. The geography of the area really wasn't changed, but the invitation to return home was no less magnificent. There's a slight shift of emphasis here with the phrase "in the desert." Now you have to pay close attention to notice it. The passage in the Hebrew version of Isaiah speaks of a voice, which would be the voice of a herald announcing the arrival of a king, which was a common custom at that time. The voice cries out: "in the desert prepare the way of the Lord." The Lord himself would come to lead his people home through desert wilderness, which was to be appropriately prepared for this journey.

The Greek version of Isaiah is punctuated differently, where it says: "A voice cries out in the desert: 'prepare the way of the Lord.'" This shows how a later inspired writer can see new meaning in a Scripture passage. John the Baptist took this second interpretation "a voice cries out in the desert: prepare the way of the Lord" and applied it to himself. This would make sense for John the Baptist to define himself in this way since he lived and preached in the desert wilderness of Judea as the gospels tell us. My father used this passage to describe himself; whenever he thought we were not agreeing with him or listening to him he used to say: "I'm just 'a voice crying out in the wilderness' and no one pays any attention to me." In John's case, a lot of people listened and responded. He was very popular and was even considered by many to be the Messiah. But he knew who he was and he claimed to be simply a messenger with the message: "prepare the way of the Lord." The Lord himself was coming to save his people and John was his herald.

The liturgy during Advent takes up the theme of John and applies it to us as we prepare to celebrate the birth of our Savior, Jesus. John, the ascetic that he was, wasn't talking about buying gifts or having parties, as enjoyable as this might be. If we read the gospels, we find out what John was talking about: repentance, changing our hearts; not taking our faith for granted or the fact that we can simply call ourselves Christians or Catholics, but living a good life and doing good works. We'll hear some more of the things he preached when we hear next Sunday's gospel. John spoke the truth and didn't mince words and that's what got him into trouble and led to his execution by Herod Antipas.

Our liturgy wants us to ask ourselves today what we need to do to live more fully as God wants us to. Jesus came to guide us to our true home. The Jews who were in Babylon for 50 years, for the most part, had never seen the land their parents and grandparents had to leave behind. They knew Babylon was not their true home. Even though we've never seen it, our true home is to be with God in eternal life. This is where the Lord is trying to take us. We know our time in this world is limited. St. Paul tells us "our citizenship is in heaven." It's where we all want to go, but not many of us are in a hurry to get there. It's up to us to prepare the way so the Lord can take us there. If we resist his lead, we'll lose out on the purpose for which God created us – to be with him. That would be the greatest tragedy that could ever happen to any of us. I would like to make a special plug for our Holy Hours on Wednesday morning and Friday afternoon and for our Solemn Annual Eucharistic Devotions which take place next weekend. Adoration of Jesus in the Blessed Sacrament would certainly help us with our spiritual preparations for Christmas. May all the prophets, and especially John the Baptist, help us to know what Advent is all about. May their message of hope and their call to prepare be more than just a voice crying out in the wilderness. Amen.

# Feast of the Immaculate Conception
## December 8, 2009

HOMILY – (Genesis 3: 9-15,20; Ephesians 1:3-6,11-12; Luke 1: 26-38) In the first three chapters of the book of Genesis, we hear about the creation of the world and all things in it. The story of creation is not meant to be a documentary that gives us an accurate historical or scientific account. It's not something that was witnessed by CNN and is now being reported on. It is a theology lesson put in story form that tells us as much about God as it does about creation. There are really two stories about creation. The first story puts God's work in the framework of seven days while the second story is more focused on the creation of our first parents and their relationship with God. It was a beautiful, loving and harmonious relationship they had with God until the devil came along disguised as a serpent. The devil was jealous of our first parents and their closeness to God, so the devil talked them into rebelling against God. Thus as St. Paul said: "sin entered into the world," a sin that seems to have become part of our DNA. This is what we call "Original Sin." It's not like some "thing" attached to us, rather it is more like a lack of something, something important is missing, which is the original grace which God blessed us with at the time of creation. This Original Sin is a kind of tendency in all of us to pride, selfishness, self-centeredness. It leads us to rebel against God like our first parents did. We see signs of it everywhere. If we read the whole passage in Genesis, we see that sin affected not only our first parents' relationship with God, but it affected their relationship with each other – they felt shame in the presence of one another. It affected their relationship with the rest of creation – they lost the joy they had in the Garden of

Eden and had to struggle with the rest of creation in order to survive. Our first reading does not go into all that. The part of the story that we heard in our first reading has the purpose of pointing out to us that, although we sin, God does not want us to remain in a state of alienation from him. Instead God would rescue the human race from this predicament we find ourselves in. So what we heard in our first reading was an announcement of good news for all of us. God spoke to the serpent, the devil, the evil one and said: "I will put enmity between you and the woman, between your offspring and hers." Enmity: in other words, all our lives we would be struggling with evil. In a poetic way God announces that evil would not win in the struggle. He told the serpent: you might strike at his heel (i.e. you might be able to do some harm to the offspring of the woman) but he will strike at your head (which would imply a fatal blow). The powers of evil will not triumph even though they often seem to. Yet sin is a powerful force, one that humanity is unable to conquer by its own power, its own cleverness, its own politics, its own laws. And so God sent his Son to come to our rescue. God's Son took on our human nature to show us the way back to a loving and harmonious relationship with God. He came to us through a woman whose goodness and holiness was not tainted by this sin that touches all the rest of us. She was full of grace from the very first moment of her existence. God did not think it fitting for the mother of his Son to be touched by sin for she would give birth to the One who would destroy sin and death in us by his own death and resurrection. When Mary was asked if she would be the mother of our Savior and Lord she answered: "May it be done to me according to your word." The answer she gave was the way she lived her whole life: always ready to say "yes" to whatever God asked of her. And so Jesus came to us, he was born, he taught, he healed, he forgave sins, he cast out demons, he died for us. Before he left us to return to the Father he gave us the sacraments to help us overcome sin and to be renewed in God's life. As we honor the Immaculate Virgin Mary, we pray she may inspire us and help us to stay close to God and in his grace by always saying "yes" to God as she did. Amen.

# 3rd Sunday of Advent
## December 13, 2009

**INTRODUCTION** – (Zephaniah 3:14-18; Philippians 4:4-7; Luke 3:10-18) Our theme for today, as it often is, is summed up in the Psalm Refrain: "Cry out with joy and gladness, for among you is the great and holy one of Israel." Our first reading from the prophet Zephaniah goes back about 700 years before Christ. The Assyrians were the dominant force in the Middle East and were an unusually warlike, brutal people. Their capital city was in northern Iraq near modern day Mosul. Our first reading comes from a time shortly after the Assyrians wiped out the northern part of Israel. They brought severe suffering upon the southern part of Israel too, the area around Jerusalem, but they did not conquer it. Jerusalem would still be around for another 130 years until the Babylonians conquered it. But the Assyrians did inflict a lot of pain on Jerusalem. Yet Jerusalem didn't learn from what happened to them. Idolatry and immorality were rampant among the Jews. The king of Judah himself offered his own son as a human sacrifice to the pagan gods. Most of what is written in the Book of Zephaniah records his efforts to correct abuses among God's people. His book ends on a note of hope, however, as he addresses those who are faithful to God. He tells them to rejoice and assures them God will rejoice and sing too because of his love for them and for all the blessings that will be theirs. Can we imagine how beautiful it would be to hear God singing?

There is something we should be aware of when we hear the second reading too. St. Paul is sitting in prison somewhere when he wrote this, and prisons in those days were really bad. Today's prisons would look like a luxury hotel by comparison. Yet Paul can be joyful and he is able to encourage the Philippians to have no anxiety and to rejoice always.

**HOMILY** – In the days when we had Mass in Latin, today was known as Gaudete Sunday. That means "Be Joyful." The liturgy continues to communicate that theme of joy with rose colored vestments and readings telling us to rejoice. So on this Gaudete Sunday, I thought we should start off with a couple of laughs.

First is about a guy driving down a country road and hears a loud thud. He gets out of the car and there is not another car in sight. So he drives on home. The next day the sheriff shows up at his door and arrests him for a hit and run accident. He ran over a pig and didn't stop and that was against the law. He protested it wasn't him and asked the sheriff how he could possibly know he was guilty. The sheriff said: "the pig squealed."

The local minister had to give a talk at a banquet and told a few funny stories. There was a news reporter there taking notes. The minister planned to give the same talk the next day at a meeting and asked the reporter not to print his jokes and stories in the newspaper the next day. So the well-meaning reporter ended his article with the following observation: "The minister told a few stories that cannot be published."

It's good to have a sense of humor and enjoy a few laughs but it's even better to have a sense of joy in our hearts. Laughter may fade away, but joy stays with us. We heard the prophet Zephaniah in today's first reading telling God's people, during an especially difficult time in their history, to "sing for joy." They should sing for joy, not because things were wonderful, but because God was in their midst. We heard Paul, in prison, telling the Philippians to rejoice always. If we listen to the media, we get the impression that joy springs from having lots of things. The scriptures tell us our joy comes from knowing the Lord is in our midst. We have an advantage over the Jews of Zephaniah's time (700 years before Christ) because we also know and believe we will enjoy being with God for all eternity. The Jews had no knowledge of heaven or hell at that time, so we have more reasons to rejoice than even holy prophets.

If we don't have joy within us, perhaps some of these enemies of joy might be at work stealing it from us:

* Feeling sorry for oneself.

* Constantly putting other people down to make ourselves look smarter or better.

* Putting ourselves down all the time. Because we're human we all make mistakes or do wrong. There are healthy ways of dealing with guilt or shame. Incidentally, the sacrament of confession is one of those ways – and this week we have four priests to hear confession at our Penance Service. Constantly beating ourselves up, though, does not get rid of guilt and it does not help us experience joy.

* Holding on to anger and resentment. It only eats us up inside and does not produce joy. We have to forgive.

* Thinking that having more things is going to make us happy. It satisfies us only momentarily.

\* And then there's fear and worry. Paul says have no anxiety at all. That might sound impossible, but there are ways we create anxiety for ourselves that we do not need. On the other hand there are many things that cause us anxiety, which we can do nothing about and we have to leave in God's hands.

If self pity, guilt, unforgiveness, anger, resentment, fear, and worry work against our having joy, then what will lead to joy? We must choose to be joyful. Paul tells the Philippians "rejoice" as if it is something for them to choose to do rather than it being something that just happens to them. I think it was Abraham Lincoln who said most people are about as happy as they make up their minds to be. Dr. Hans Selye, the scientist who developed and researched the concept of stress, would agree. He said: it's generally not the things outside of us that create stress for us, but it's the way we respond to these things. Next we need to be good and to do good. Otherwise we won't feel good about ourselves. The people in today's gospel ask the Baptist, "what should we do?" John gave them a few specific ideas. All we have to do is read the gospels or the 10 Commandments and we'll get the idea that there's more to a good life than just saying "I believe!" Lastly, I think gratitude is the final key to unlocking the way to joy. Again, being grateful is an intentional thing; it is an attitude we must develop. St. Paul said: "in everything, by prayer and petition, with thanksgiving, make your requests known to God." A heart that is ungrateful is not happy. This is not all that could be said about joy, but it's probably enough for us to think about today. My closing words for today are don't make yourselves so anxious this season that you lose the joy that can be found only in knowing Jesus' love. "The Lord, your God, is in your midst."

# 4th Sunday of Advent
## December 20, 2009

INTRODUCTION – (Micah 5:1-4a; Hebrews 10:5-10; Luke 1:39-45) Approximately 700 years before Christ, the Assyrian's were the dominant power in the Middle East. Their capital was in what is today, northern Iraq. The Assyrian army was powerful and was legendary for its savagery. After they had destroyed the northern half of Israel, they moved against Jerusalem. Naturally the citizens of Jerusalem were terrified. We hear in today's first reading words of hope spoken to God's people by the prophet Micah. He promises salvation would come out of an unimportant little village about seven miles south of Jerusalem named Bethlehem. This prophecy from Micah was the Old Testament passage the Jewish leaders quoted when the Magi came to Jerusalem looking for the newborn king of the Jews. Bethlehem had been the birthplace of King David 300 years before the prophet Micah. According to the prophet it would be the birthplace of the future savior of God's people whose greatness would reach to the ends of the earth. What an amazing prophecy coming from 700 years before Christ and what an amazing way in which God fulfilled it!

HOMILY – You can tell we are getting near Christmas by the traditional greeting that shoppers give each other in the mall: "I think I was next."

Red Skelton's recipe for a good marriage was: "We always hold hands. If I let go, she shops."

After the angel appeared to Mary and announced to her that God wanted her to be the mother of the long awaited Messiah, the angel informed Mary that her aged relative, Elizabeth, who had wanted all her life to have a baby was now going to have one. Mary, St. Luke tells us, traveled in haste to be with her relative.

Elizabeth's having a child at an advanced age was a sign that, as the angel said to Mary, "nothing is impossible with God." It was also a sign that her child would be very special. Remember Sara, wife of Abraham, did not have a child until she was well advanced in age. This was also the true of the mother of Samson and Hanna, the mother of the prophet Samuel. Elizabeth's child, John the Baptist, indeed was a special person. He was to be the one to announce the coming of the Messiah, and already, before his birth he shows signs of his special role as he leaps for joy as Mary, and Jesus within her, approaches.

Notice the greeting of Elizabeth: "blessed are you among women and blessed is the fruit of your womb." That greeting along with the greeting of the angel to Mary at the annunciation: "Hail, full of grace, the Lord is with you," makes up the first part of the Hail Mary – a prayer that took its present form about 1000 years ago.

The part of this gospel that struck me was the statement that after Elizabeth's child leapt for joy, Elizabeth was filled with the Holy Spirit. This enabled her to recognize Mary's secret and greet her as she did: Blessed are you among women and blessed is the fruit of your womb. Mary had just been visited by the angel. Remember, Luke said she went with haste to visit Elizabeth. There would be no evidence that she had conceived, but Elizabeth knew it. It was because she had been filled with the Holy Spirit.

Jesus comes to us in so many ways, but without the Holy Spirit we are unable to recognize him. But when the Holy Spirit enlightens us, we know the Spirit is present. The Spirit helps us see him present in creation, in the Eucharist, in one another, in perhaps the person who drives us crazy, in the poor and suffering and in the unborn who are like Jesus was at that moment in Mary, entirely vulnerable, without a voice to speak or cry out.

One example of how the Holy Spirit helped me to know the presence of Jesus was in the Scriptures. So many times I have experienced reading the Scriptures and a particular verse spoke to me with such power that I knew instinctively it was something Jesus wanted me to hear and learn from. It spoke to me not, just in my head as a thought, but it spoke in my heart as something I could feel with my whole being. I still remember the first time it happened. I was in my first year in the seminary, feeling somewhat lonely and homesick, and I just opened the Scriptures to Matthew. I read where Jesus said, "All the hairs on your head are counted. So do not be afraid." (Mt. 10:30-31) Immediately I felt God's love and my troubled mood lifted. That's just one example of many times I've experienced our Lord through the Spirit.

As we celebrate the last week of Advent, may we be inspired by the Spirit to see beyond all the busyness and stress at this time and know the presence of Jesus with us as we celebrate his birth. Amen.

## Christmas
### December 25, 2009

HOMILY – On Christmas night the local minister's wife collapsed on the couch and said to her husband "I am really exhausted." He said "You're exhausted! How about me? I had two Christmas Eve services and three services this morning to do; that's five sermons. Why are you so tired?" She replied: "I had to listen to all of them, dear!" (from *The Joyful Noiseletter*, Dec. 2000)

I would like to offer a few suggestions for Christmas gifts: To one who has hurt you: forgiveness. To someone who drives you crazy: tolerance and patience. To a friend: your heart. To a customer: service. To all: charity. To every child: good example. To yourself: respect. (adapted from *Chicken Soup for the Soul, Christmas Treasury*, pg 63)

It's instinctive for us to come together on this feast of our Lord's birth. It helps us to get to the heart of what all our other celebrations are all about and, in this gift giving season, to thank God for the greatest gift any of us could receive, the gift of God's love shown to us in the coming of Jesus into our lives.

If I tried to put into words the wonder of the mystery we celebrate, I would fail because the mystery of God's love and the gift of Jesus to us is beyond what words can describe. That's one reason we come to Mass every week – to try, in whatever little way we can, to grasp the awesomeness of the coming of our Savior to us. Because stories seem to touch us at a deeper level than other words, we often resort to telling stories at this time.

So my story takes place on Christmas day way out west in California. (story can be found in *A World of Stories for Preachers and Teachers* by William J. Bausch, pg 458) This Christmas day occurred a few years ago on a Sunday. A family, mother, father and three children, 10, 6 and an infant one year old were traveling from St. Francisco along the California coast to Los Angeles. They lived in Los Angeles and had been visiting family members in San Francisco. It happened that Dennis, the father, had to be at work on Monday morning and that's why they were on the road going home on Christmas day. Mom tells the story. When it got later in the afternoon, we looked for a restaurant and felt lucky to find one that was open on Christmas. There were just a few people in the restaurant when we all came in. We got settled at a table and ordered. Suddenly our one year old, Christopher, started getting very excited. He let out a few joyful squeals and started pounding on his metal high chair with his fat little hands. His eyes were wide open and his toothless mouth opened into a big grin. Mom continues on: I started looking around to see what was exciting Christopher and half way to the door sat the object of his excitement, a bum with grimy, dirty clothes, needing a shave, worn out baggy pants and shoes and the appearance that maybe he had had a couple too many beers. I found him repulsive but there he was, waving across the room at Christopher, shouting "hi there big fella." Suddenly he started playing: "Peek a boo" and "Patty cake." Christopher really enjoyed all the attention while the rest of us were totally embarrassed. The few other people in the restaurant looked annoyed. We finished dinner in record time as all this was going on and Dennis went to pay the bill. I gathered Christopher in my arms and headed toward the door – but I had to pass the old man and prayed I could get by him without incident. Christopher, however, had his eyes riveted on his new best friend and when I got near the old man Christopher almost jumped out of my arms with his arms outstretched. For just a split second, I noticed the man's eyes, beseeching me to let him hold Christopher. I handed him to the man and he held Christopher so gently. The man's eyes were closed and there were a few tears on his cheeks as he cradled and rocked Christopher in his arms for a few moments. Christopher didn't want to leave, but the man gave him back to me. He said "God bless you, Ma'am. You've just made my Christmas. Take good care of him." A little choked up, I said I would and left him saying to myself "God forgive me."

A little baby comes to us tonight with his arms outstretched to embrace us in our sad state, with our tattered lives, our tattered hurts, our tattered relationships and our tattered sins. He embraces us by taking on our human flesh; he embraces us in accepting poverty and suffering to save us; he embraces us by giving himself to us in the sacrament of the Eucharist.

If we are here tonight knowing we have been embraced by Christ's love, and if, like the rag-tag shepherds that we are, we are here rejoicing and praising God for his love, then we have captured the mystery of Christmas: God-with-us, Emmanuel, has loved us greatly. May you experience the peace, love, comfort and joy of God's embrace this day and throughout this Christmas season. Amen.

# Holy Family
## December 27, 2009

HOMILY – (Sirach 3:2-6, 12-14; Colossians 3:12-21; Luke 2:41-52) Just a few days ago we heard St. Luke describe the birth of Jesus at Bethlehem. Although the manger may not have been the Ritz, we imagined a scene described in the song: Silent night, Holy night. The silence of that night was broken only by the angels praising God and announcing peace to God's people on earth. Now we hear Matthew's gospel. The peace and quiet are gone. The paranoid king, Herod the Great, is intent on destroying the child Jesus and the Holy Family have to escape by leaving their own homeland and becoming refugees in neighboring Egypt. It's like a splash of cold water in the face, but this splash is really a splash of cold reality, reminding us that no family, not even the holiest has a stress-free existence. It also reminds us of the universal conflict and tension between the forces of good and evil, light and darkness, grace and sin. The forces of evil lined up against Jesus right from the beginning. Matthew's story also reminds us that although our decision to follow Jesus takes us along a road that leads to eternal happiness, that road is not always a paved or smooth.

Our focus today is on the family. The importance of the family cannot be overstated or over emphasized. The family is where we discover what it means to be human, what are our strengths and weaknesses, where we experience love and forgiveness, where we learn about relationships, unity, sacrifice, loving others, accepting others, where we learn values and attitudes and trust and how to handle stress and how to be responsible. Family is where we learn how to get along with one another. All these important learning tasks are hopefully learned in a family that is relatively healthy. I say "relatively healthy" because none of us and none of our families are perfect. A family that is seriously dysfunctional teaches a lot of other things that end up not being very helpful. The success of society depends depend on the health of the family. That creates a big burden for families to carry. It also puts a big burden on society to care about the family and to foster healthy families.

Today we celebrate the importance of another family, our parish family. Here too we discover who we are as God's children, how to trust God and to love God and one another. We learn values here too, values that are intended to lead us into eternal life. Hopefully we learn how to give as well as take, how to forgive as well as be forgiven. Here we gather around a family table to be fed, not with perishable food but with food that will nourish us eternally. Our faith community is just as important in its own way as our family of origin. And the Lord's supper that we share is just as important to our spiritual well being as being together and eating together as a family is to our emotional well being.

Today we celebrate 10 years as the united family of
St. Boniface and St. Patrick. Back in 1853 St. Aloysius
was founded as the Catholic parish in North Side. It
didn't last as such. The area grew and there was not
always peace between the Irish and the Germans, so in
less than 10 years St. Aloysius became two parishes: St.
Boniface and St. Patrick. On December 29, 1991 we
formally became once again, a single parish. Since St.
Boniface was structurally the stronger of the two and
since St. Boniface had a school, St. Patrick parishioners
moved here and the move was a good one from
practically every aspect. Only a hand full of people that
I know of were unhappy about the merger. (We put
passed out a booklet a few years ago which contains
much more history about our parish. Most people
probably already have one, but if you do not we have
some more at the doors of church.)

It has been my privilege to be pastor here for the ten
years since our merger. None of us knows what the future
holds, but if I could make a guess, I think for many reasons
St. Boniface will be here for a long time. As for myself, if
my health holds up and if the Archbishop lets me I would
like to be here for at least another six years. By then I will
be 70. I do not know what I will do when I turn 70. I
will have to reevaluate things when I get there.

I do want to say how grateful I am to have so many
people's support. There's only one thing I wish, and that
is that more people took seriously the serious obligation
to attend Mass weekly. I think that for the most part
families are strengthened by meals together. And the
Lord's supper is our family meal each week. I have seen
too many people, once they get away from going to Mass
every week, slowly drift away from their faith. St. Paul
gives us a wonderful list of virtues that would enhance
and enrich any of our relationships with one another,

especially the relationships within our families: compassion, kindness, gentleness, humility, patience, forgiveness, etc. Notice in this short passage he tells us twice to be grateful. The words St. Paul wrote of course were Greek, but you might find it instructive to hear what words he used: the verb he used was "Eucharisteo." And he tells us we are to become "Eucharistos." It is obvious from these words that the Eucharist allows us to perfectly fulfill his mandate. It is a perfect act of thanksgiving because, in a special way, we, as God's sons and daughters, offer thanks in union with God's own Son, Jesus Christ. May we, on this anniversary, give thanks for our family in Christ, and for our own immediate families. May we be strong and healthy families, full of thankfulness, and may we rejoice one day in the home of the one Father we all have in common, our Father in heaven. Amen.

# Mary Mother of God
## January 1, 2010

HOMILY – (Numbers 6:22-27; Galatians 4:4-7; Luke 2:16-21) I entertained myself this afternoon looking up information about the new year. I've always wondered how January 1 became New Year's Day. I wondered how other cultures celebrate New Year's. I've always known that the Jewish new year begins on Rosh Hashanah which will fall on September 18, 2009. I've always known that the Chinese have their own new year celebration which this year will be Jan. 26, 2009. Because their calendar is a little shorter than ours, the Moslems began two new years' in 2008; one in January and another in December. But I was amazed to see all the other cultures that have their own new year at different times and seasons. January 1 was chosen as the start of the new year by the early Romans in 153 BCE. Prior to that date they celebrated the new year in the spring which seems logical since nature starts to come alive at that time. But in 153 BCE the Roman senate chose January 1 as the beginning of a new year because that was the day when the Roman consuls took office. The date is quite arbitrary. It is said they celebrated with "boisterous joy, superstitious practices and gross orgies." The early Christians made January 1 a day of penance as a reaction against the excesses of the pagans. Eventually it was made a feast of Mary as the "Mother of God." I learned too that many European countries didn't officially make January 1 the start of the new year until the 16th, 17th, and 18th centuries. Now practically all big cities of the world celebrate January 1 even if they have their own new year, like China.

The Church's celebration of the new year is the first Sunday of Advent. It makes little reference to January 1 as the start of a new year as it falls during the octave of Christmas. Christmas is too important a feast for just a one-day celebration, so the liturgy celebrates Christmas solemnly for eight days. After today, the liturgy continues to celebrate Christmas, but less solemnly, until the feast of the Baptism of our Lord. Although the angel had already told Joseph that Mary's son was to be named Jesus, today also recalls the day on which Jesus was circumcised and officially given his name. We might reflect for a moment how respectful we are of this name by which we are to be saved. Pope Paul VI asked that today be observed as a day of prayer for peace, which is so badly needed in today's world.

As we celebrate the beginning of 2009 we are hopeful nations might find a better way than waging war to get along with one another. We are hopeful also that our world will be more just, that life will be respected, that we might enjoy health and happiness. Although we may party at this time of year, we also have a lot of reasons to be here in church, to seek God's help in the coming year, and to thank him for his help in the past.

Mary, the Mother of God and our spiritual mother gives us an example of how to enter into this new year. We are told she reflected on all these events in her heart. What events? The annunciation by the angel, the visit to her cousin Elizabeth, Jesus' birth, the visit by the shepherds and the magi. May we too continue to reflect on them in our hearts. The rosary can help us in this. May we come to know God's support as we move another year closer to the kingdom of his eternal love. Amen.

# Feast of the Epiphany
## January 3, 2010

**INTRODUCTION** – (Isaiah 60:1-6; Ephesians 3:2-3a; Matthew 2:1-12) 587 years before Christ, Jerusalem was destroyed by the Babylonians. Fifty years later, the Persians (people living in modern day Iran) conquered the Babylonians, and they allowed the Jews to return home. Some of my friends had a fire recently and I see the stress they are going through trying to recover from it. I cannot imagine the difficulties and stresses the Jewish people were under as they tried to rebuild their homes, their Temple, their farms 50 years after everything had been destroyed. The prophet in today's first reading tries to encourage God's people and assure them Jerusalem would again be a great city. He sees Jerusalem becoming a light for all the world. His vision is that people would come from distant places to visit Jerusalem to be nourished by the radiant light of God's presence. St. Matthew sees the vision of the prophet fulfilled in the birth of Jesus and the visit of the magi.

HOMILY – Today we hear the story of the magi, mysterious visitors to the Christ child who came from the East. They are often called kings, based on the words of the prophet in our first reading and from the psalm refrain that followed, but most scholars tell us they were probably priests of an eastern religion called Zoroastrianism. Zoroaster, who lived about 1000 years before Christ, taught that there are two gods, the god of light who created all that is good and an evil god, a god of darkness who creates all that is evil in the world. Astrology was mixed in with the belief of the magi in that they apparently believed that every great person had a guiding light in heaven, which appeared as a star, and the greater the person, the brighter the star. Matthew doesn't tell us how many magi came to visit our Lord. The number three that is part of our tradition is based on the number of gifts they brought.

It recently struck me how the story of the magi has many similarities to our coming to Mass each week. They saw a star and they realized there was a meaning behind it and went searching to see what they could find. It is normal for all of us at times to experience some natural wonder, the stars perhaps, or a beautiful sunset or the birth of a child and to get a sense there is something or someone even more wondrous behind our spiritually moving experience. Our Mass brings us together with other searchers, others who seek to know, for example, the meaning of our existence, the reason for suffering, the way to peace and joy.

One of the things that guided the magi in the right direction was the scriptures. Notice that almost the whole first half hour of the Mass centers around the scriptures. It would have been natural for the magi to expect that the newborn king of the Jews would be born in the great capital of the Jewish people, maybe even in the household of the current king of the Jews, king Herod. But no, the prophet Micah points them in the right direction. The bible is our basic guide in life, giving us our knowledge about God, about creation, about ourselves, and about how to live. Unfortunately, those who knew the bible, the Jewish chief priests and scribes didn't benefit from what they knew. They gave correct information, but didn't follow it themselves. That can happen in the Church as well, Church leaders may know what's right and wrong but not live it. That's why we must pray for our spiritual leaders. I try as hard as I can to give good guidance when I give a homily, but I also will be accountable as to how well I live what I preach.

The magi brought gifts for the newborn king. You bring gifts too: your time, your attentive presence, your participation, your financial support. In connection with that I want to thank our parishioners for their response to my appeal a few weeks ago for increased giving. We are getting out of the hole we started to get into and perhaps we'll even regain some of the deficit we accumulated last fiscal year. Your response has been most gratifying and I am most grateful.

When the magi found the child, he did not appear to be anyone spectacular. He wasn't dressed in royal robes or living in a palace or even in a prestigious city. His parents weren't noteworthy and wealthy citizens. The magi found an ordinary little baby but they knew, through the guidance they had received, he was special. When we come to Mass, we know Christ is with us, but we don't see anything special. We see others like ourselves, we see a priest, we see an altar and statues and candles, we see what appears to be bread and wine,

but we believe it is much more. We believe we have
found the Lord and yet we know our search is not over.
There are greater things ahead.

One last comment. As I said earlier, we don't know
how many magi there were, but there was more than
one. Travel was dangerous and people always traveled
in groups. Even today we need to come together with
others because we need one another's support and
prayers and inspiration. As Thomas Merton said, we
don't get to heaven by ourselves. We need each other's
help. May our journey this year lead us to know and
love the infinite Son of God who came to lead us to
eternal life. Amen.

# Baptism of the Lord
## January 10, 2010

**INTRODUCTION** – (Isaiah 42:1-4, 6-7; Acts 10:34-
38; Luke 3:15-16, 21-22) Many kings, prophets, and holy
people served God in Old Testament times, and must
have pleased God by their holy lives; however, in four
places in the book of the prophet Isaiah, God speaks of
someone with whom he is especially pleased. This
servant is not identified by name and, because the
passages are poetic in form, they are usually referred to as
the servant songs. They were written about 500 years
before Christ. Perhaps the passages refer to someone
who was alive at the time of the prophet, but what is
amazing is how perfectly they describe Jesus – even 500
years before he was born.

**HOMILY** – I'm sure everyone has their Christmas
decorations down by now – except the Church. The
Church continues to celebrate the feast of Christmas and
Epiphany until the feast of the Baptism of our Lord,

which is today. The word Epiphany means to reveal or to show something. God began to reveal his Son to the world with the coming of the magi, but for those who came to Mass during this past week, each day's gospel tried to show the uniqueness of Jesus. Today with the baptism of Jesus, God reveals that Jesus is filled with the Spirit and is God's beloved Son with whom God is greatly pleased.

The image that most caught my attention in reading today's gospel is when St. Luke tells us "heaven was opened." This has great symbolic meaning. St. Mark uses a stronger term in his account of the baptism of Jesus when he says, "the heavens tore apart." The Greek word Mark used is σχίξω (schidzo), a word that means "to divide by use of force, split, tear off or tear apart. This word is part of our English words: schism, schismatic, schizoid and schizophrenia.

This is why this image struck me. When we think of God, we think of him being up there and we're down here and there is always a cloud that seems to hide him from us. The clouds symbolically formed a barrier between God and us. And in many ways that's true. God is so far beyond our ability to know or understand. When the Second person of the Blessed Trinity took on our human flesh in the incarnation, the heavens were torn open. Earth was united with heaven, the barrier between God and ourselves no longer existed. When the Son of God took on our human nature, he became like us in every way except sin (as St. Paul tells us). He came to bridge the distance between God and us, and to make it possible for us to know him in a close and intimate way. We still have a long way to go in our relationship with God, but the way has been opened up for us to keep growing closer and closer. That way is Jesus.

Let me talk about how our own baptism fits into this picture. Human life begins approximately nine months prior to the birth of a child, from the moment a human egg is fertilized. Not knowing exactly when this event might occur, for millennia we have celebrated the beginning of a child's life on its day of birth. A child prior to birth is just as human as a child who has just been born, but many people refuse to accept this. Nonetheless, when human life begins, that life is the highest form of life on this planet, endowed with unalienable rights among which are life, liberty and the pursuit of happiness.

When a person is baptized, something really marvelous happens. The baptized person is lifted up to a higher level of life. He or she remains human but is made more than human. God reaches out and makes this human person his own child. We use the term "reborn." That word is literally true. God could say over the person newly baptized, "you are my beloved child. On you my favor rests." St. John says it clearly in his epistle, "See what love the Father has given us, that we should be called children of God; and that is what we are." (1 Jn 3,1) At baptism the heavens are torn open, heaven is joined to earth and the barrier between God and the one who was baptized in essence no longer exists. I say "in essence" because "in everyday experience" there is still quite a distance between God and us. The word "reborn" can help explain that reality. When a child is born, there is a lot of work ahead for the child and its parents before a person attains full maturity as a human being. Also, when we're reborn into God's life, there is a lot of work ahead for the person who has been reborn and its parents before that person attains full maturity in Christ. Birth and baptism are both indeed miracles, but both are just a beginning.

Probably most of us seldom think of baptism and what a wonderful gift of life God gave us in baptism except on a feast like we are celebrating today or at an occasional baptism of a relative. But there are things to remind us of the sacrament, such as blessing ourselves with holy water when we enter church or the baptistery and Paschal Candle here in the sanctuary. Often we do not think of this but what we do every time we come to Mass is to renew the grace of baptism, to accept again the privilege of sharing God's life, to have that life be nourished and strengthened by God's word and by receiving Jesus' body and blood in Communion. At Mass we renew our desire to live faithfully as God's son or daughter.

The Second Person of the Blessed Trinity, the Son of God, was God from all eternity and when the Son of God took on human flesh in Jesus, he was God's Son from the moment of his conception. So Jesus' baptism did not make him any more God's Son or any more filled with the Holy Spirit than he already was. When Jesus was baptized, the Father and the Spirit demonstrated what had always been. But when we are baptized we are significantly changed, we are made infinitely more than what we were. May God help us live up to our high calling. Amen.

# 2nd Sunday in Ordinary Time
## January 17, 2010

INTRODUCTION – (Isaiah 62:1-5; 1 Corinthians 12:4-11; John 2:1-11) For almost fifty years the Jews were captives and exiles in Babylon (modern day Iraq). But then the Persians (modern day Iran) conquered the Babylonians, and they allowed God's people to return home. The Persians were even willing to give them financial aid to rebuild their Temple, their homes, their cities and their farms. The prophet in today's first reading announces this wonderful event that God would bring his people back home. During their exile God had not forgotten his people and would take his people back to himself as his bride. The image of God marrying his people is an important biblical image, found in several of the prophets, and is the best symbol from our human experience that can be used to describe the affection God has for us. This wedding image prepares the way for the gospel account of Jesus' first miracle at the wedding feast of Cana.

**HOMILY** – Since our gospel is about a wedding, I want to start with a few quotes that offer some wit and wisdom about marriage. James Thurber said: "the most dangerous food is wedding cake." Ruth Graham said: "A happy marriage is the union of two forgivers." Lyndon Johnson: "Only two things are necessary to keep one's wife happy. One is to let her think she is having her own way; the other, to let her have it." Mignon McLaughlin: "A successful marriage requires falling in love many times, always with the same person." Joseph Barth: "Marriage is our last, best chance to grow up." Bill Cosby: "For two people in a marriage to live together day after day is unquestionably the one miracle the Vatican has overlooked." (quotes taken from *Readers' Digest*, 5/09, pg 184)

Since our gospel is about wine, I have a quote from Benjamin Franklin: "We hear of the conversion of water into wine as a miracle. But this conversion is, through the goodness of God, made every day before our eyes. Behold the rain which descends from heaven upon our vineyards; there it enters the roots of the vines, to be changed into wine – a constant proof that God loves us, and loves to see us happy." (from *Readers' Digest*, 6/09, pg 159)

Making wine is a lengthy process; the miracle, of course, is that Jesus made the wine instantaneously, made it of such excellent quality and in such great abundance (120 to 150 gallons). What is the point of his doing that and what is the point of this story for us? John tells us it was a sign. So it's meant to tell us something. Let us explore what the sign tells us. It was not a sign that Jesus was opening up a new wine shop in the neighborhood. His mission would not be limited to time or place. As we sang in the psalm refrain, his mission was to all nations. God's people were always praying for and looking for the day when God would come to save his people. That day was often expressed in wedding imagery (as we heard in today's first reading) and an abundance of wine would mark the arrival of that day. I would like to quote from several places in the Old Testament where an abundance of wine would be a sign of God's coming as our savior. We read in Isaiah: "On this mountain the Lord of hosts will provide for all peoples a feast of rich food and choice wines, juicy, rich food and pure, choice wines; he will destroy death forever. The Lord God will wipe away the tears from all faces. On that day it will be said: 'behold our God, to whom we looked to save us!'" (Is 25:6, 9) Or again from Isaiah: "you who have no money, come, receive grain and eat; come without paying and without cost, drink wine and milk!" (Is. 55:1) Amos tells us: "The days are coming says the Lord, when the juice of grapes shall drip down the mountains and all the hills shall run with it." (Amos 9:13) In Proverbs we read about wisdom, personified as a woman who has built her house, dressed her meat, mixed her wine and has spread her table. She sends out her maidens and calls out to the city to all who would be wise and understanding: "come, eat my food, and drink of the wine I have mixed!" (Prov. 9:1-5) Overindulgence in alcohol is foolishness and destructive, but the Jewish people have always had one of the lowest percentages of alcoholism of all nationalities. They respect its power and thus it is for them a symbol of joy and celebration and, according to their Scriptures, it is a sign of the abundance of joy with which God would bless his people on the day of salvation.

But that's not all that the miracle tells us, for, as a sign it tells us a lot of other things, such as, it was a sign of who Jesus is. It was a sign of his unique person – as John's gospel tells us: "he revealed his glory and his disciples began to believe in him." It was a sign that he was the messiah who would bring God's blessing of salvation to all God's people. Since he would be a light to all nations, as is often spoken of him, it is not just the Jewish people who would share in God's blessings. He would be a blessing for all people who would follow him. Another meaning to this sign is that this would be the beginning of Jesus' saving work, a term described as his "hour." His work would lead to his execution and his resurrection as he well knew. Perhaps knowing what was ahead for him, Jesus wasn't in a hurry to begin his work. So when his mother, Mary, described the difficult problem of not having enough wine, his response was, "my hour has not yet come." Notice she didn't push him into anything, but she probably knew he would want to help this young couple who would have been dreadfully embarrassed if their celebration came to a rapid end. Mary just said to the servants, "Do whatever he tells you." (Good advice for any and all of us.) Another sign here for me is his interest in every detail of our own lives. Did he not tell us in another place: "Are not two sparrows sold for a small coin? Yet not one of them falls to the ground without your Father's knowledge. Even all the hairs of your head are counted. (Mt. 10:29) It was a sign he came to change things: he changed sick people into people who were well, he changed sinners into saints, he changed death into a pathway into everlasting life, he changed bread and wine into his body and blood. Finally, the miracle at Cana was a sign of the Eucharist, in which he would give his blood for us, his blood, which represents his life and his blessings that are offered to those who come to be nourished by him. Amen.

## 3rd Sunday in Ordinary Time
### January 24, 2010

**INTRODUCTION** – (Neh. 8:2-4a, 5-6, 8-10; 1 Corinthians 12:12-30; Luke 1:1-4; Luke 4:14-21) After the Persians released the Jews from their Babylonian exile and even assisted them to return to their homeland, it did not happen all at once. After fifty years in Babylon, most of the Jews were quite comfortable there and were not in a hurry to return to their devastated homeland. Even a hundred years after being allowed to go back to Israel, they continued to struggle in their efforts to rebuild their cities and their civilization. Today's first reading brings us back to that period of return and restoration, about 100 years after the Jews started returning home. The Persians were still the reigning power in the Middle East – including Israel. Today's first reading is from the book of Nehemiah. Nehemiah had held an important position as a servant to the Persian king. Knowing the difficulties the Jews were confronted with, the king allowed Nehemiah to return to Israel to help his people rebuild and appointed Nehemiah to be governor in Israel. In an effort to rebuild the nation, Nehemiah started with what was most important and that was their faith in God. In today's first reading Nehemiah called for a general assembly of the people and he delegated the priest-scribe, Ezra, to read God's word to them. Remember, books were very rare in those days and were very expensive, since there were no printing presses. Every letter of every word had to be individually printed by a scribe. Very few people knew how to either read or write. So, for an ordinary person to know God's word, someone had to read it or preach it to them. Ezra read God's word to the people and interpreted it for them. The reading was most probably from the first five books of the bible. Notice how the people actively responded to God's word.

**HOMILY** – The people who heard God's word in our first reading and in our gospel took what they heard seriously. If they hadn't taken it seriously, their response would have been indifference. They were certainly not indifferent to the Word. Unfortunately, the people of Nazareth eventually responded to Jesus with hostility, which was not the response Jesus was looking for. One of the questions I have been hearing frequently from people who want to take Jesus' words seriously is if the Bible is God's word, how did it come to be. Did it come floating down out of heaven? Well, no. I want to explain today the gospels and how they came to be. I'm not going to try to explain the development of the Hebrew Bible or what we call the Old Testament. That would take quite a long time. I am probably biting off more than I should in even trying to explain the development of the gospels, but we get some special help today from St. Luke. That is why I am bringing up this topic for my homily. I don't think it's something I've ever preached on before. Luke tells us at the very beginning of his gospel why he wrote what he did and how he went about it. He gives us a similar introduction at the beginning of his second work, the Acts of the Apostles.

Most of you probably know that the gospels were not written until many years after Jesus died and rose. So how did people learn about Jesus? Many knew him during his lifetime. He was a public figure, teaching and healing for about three years. Immediately after the Spirit came upon the Apostles at Pentecost, they began to tell the story of Jesus. In spite of persecution, and actually because many believers fled the persecutions, the story of Jesus quickly spread all through the Middle East and the Mediterranean area. The Acts of the Apostles and the Letters of Paul give us some idea of how this process took place so quickly. As the Apostles traveled far and wide, as faith began to grow, and as those who were eyewitnesses to Jesus began to die out or be put to death, the need for authoritative written accounts of Jesus' life and teachings increased. Because of the striking similarities between the first three gospels, scholars reasonably assume there was a collection of Jesus' sayings which they call Q, which stands for the word Quelle (the German word for source). Whatever document contained this collection of Jesus' sayings no longer exists, but it was available in the early Church. The earliest document we have about Jesus is not a gospel. It is Paul's first letter to the Thessalonians and was written about 51 A.D. The earliest gospel, St. Mark, came on the scene 20 years later – around the year 70. Matthew and Luke were written about the year 85 A.D. It is easy to picture Matthew and Luke each having the gospel of Mark in front of them as they composed their own gospels for they borrow heavily from Mark. But they each had other sources as well to help them put their gospels together. As we just heard Luke tell us at the beginning of his gospel, others "have undertaken to compile a narrative of the events that have been fulfilled among us, just as those who were eyewitnesses from the beginning and ministers of the word have handed them down to us." Luke evidentially feels he has some things to say that the others didn't say – and indeed he did have a lot to tell us that the others didn't. Luke goes on to tell us he very carefully investigated everything and wrote it down so that Theophilus might be strengthened in faith regarding the teachings he was already familiar with – through other writings and preaching. The name Theophilus means "friend of God" so he could have been a real person or the name could symbolize all of us. Just to deviate from Luke for a moment, John tells us he wrote his gospel for the same reason, so that we may believe in Jesus as Messiah and Son of God and through this belief we may have life in his name. (Jn 20:31) John assures us that his testimony is that of an eyewitness. (Jn 19:35) By the way, John's gospel is believed to have been written roughly around the same period as Matthew and Luke (or maybe later). Other gospels came to be written too. I have a list of 16 other gospels, most of which came out of heretical groups and were from a later time. Most are in Greek. I have a copy of some that were published in English. I confess I didn't read much from them. I found them boring and at times somewhat bizarre. They really do not reflect the belief of the early Church about Christ and that's why they pretty much were ignored or forgotten. What we have in the four gospels reflects the belief of the early Christians as derived from the apostles and from eyewitnesses. It is the testimony of men and women who were willing to give up their life rather than give up, not just what they believed, but what they had seen. As John says in his first letter: the Word of life was made visible; "we have seen it and testify to it and proclaim to you the eternal life that was with the Father and was made visible to us..." *(1 John 1:2)* Matthew, Mark, Luke and John all give us the same message of faith about Jesus, but they are four different authors so they describe Jesus in their own unique way and with their own unique emphasis. We can learn from each of them, and we do throughout our three-year liturgical cycle. When we read what their words, God is speaking to us through them. May the seriousness of their message lead us to respond with faith and love to the Word we hear. Amen.

## 4th Sunday in Ordinary Time
### January 31, 2010

INTRODUCTION – (Jeremiah 1:4-5, 17-19; 1 Cor. 12:31-13:13; Lk 4:21-30) As St. Luke begins his gospel, he tells **why** he wrote it and **how** he went about it. We heard that last week. Then he goes on to tell us the beautiful stories about the birth of John the Baptist and Jesus and about how Jesus was lost in the Temple when he was twelve years old. We are not told what else happened to Jesus as he was growing up. Since it was the custom in those days, we can only assume that he worked with his father as a craftsman. About the age of thirty, Jesus was baptized by John in the Jordan then was led by the Spirit into the desert to fast and pray for 40 days. Luke then begins to tell us about Jesus' ministry of teaching and healing and his visit to his hometown of Nazareth. As a devout person, Jesus went to the synagogue faithfully on the Sabbath and was invited to do a reading from the prophet Isaiah and teach on it. This is where last Sunday's gospel ended. Today we hear how his relatives and former neighbors responded to his message – with enthusiasm at first, but it turned into hostility. Our first reading, as usual, prepares us for the gospel. Jeremiah the prophet heard God's call to preach, a job that God warned him would lead to suffering and rejection.

**HOMILY** – Overheard in a restaurant: a lady was telling her friend, "my husband and I had a big argument and we ended up not talking to one another for three days. Finally, on the third day he asked where one of his shirts was. I said 'So, now you're talking to me.' He looked confused and asked 'What are you talking about?' I said, 'haven't you noticed I haven't spoken to you for three days?' He said: 'No, I just thought we were getting along.'" (from *Reader's Digest book, Laughter – the Best Medicine*) Such is the joy and complexity of love. I'll say something about that later. But first, today's gospel.

We are left with a lot of questions. How is it that Jesus' visit to his hometown turned from enthusiasm to such hostility they wanted to kill him? Or how did he get away from them without being harmed? Is Luke telling us, in summarized form, what took place over the course of a number of visits Jesus made to Nazareth as he began his ministry? Luke doesn't answer our concerns. The only detail he gives us is that the people didn't consider Jesus anyone special – even though they were already familiar with stories of his miraculous powers. I think St. Luke is giving us a warning of what was ahead for Jesus: how his ministry of teaching and healing started out to be very popular with the people. Gradually, as people, especially some of the Jewish leaders, really started to understand his message, opposition to him grew until he was put to death. Perhaps Luke is teaching us that we can't take Jesus on our terms but on his terms; we can't make Jesus into who we would like him to be. We must accept him on the basis of who he want us to be. Perhaps Luke is also showing us that Jesus was not a politician who tried to cater to people's wants; he was a prophet who would be faithful to the mission God sent him on, no matter what the consequences were.

Our second reading from St. Paul is one of the most beautiful passages written by him. It is especially popular at weddings, and rightly so. It may sound romantic, and indeed a couple who loves one another in the way Paul describes love would surely not lose the romance in their relationship. But the love Paul talks about does not happen easily or without effort. It demands discipline, unselfishness and self-sacrifice. As Paul says, love is not self-seeking; he insists that without love we are nothing. Paul means this literally. His argument for this statement comes one chapter earlier in his letter when he compares the Christian Community to the body of Christ. We are all a part of that body and none of us can say we can get along without the other members of the body. It's like our own body. It has many parts, and each part functions because it is part of the whole. If our arm were cut off it may have the appearance of an arm, but literally it would not be an arm. It would be a mass of bone and skin and flesh. It's only an arm when it is connected to the body, which gives it its life and it's ability to function. Without its connection to the body, it is nothing. What connects us with one another and makes us one body is love. Without love we are separate individuals, no longer one with our head, which is Christ, and no longer one with each other. Thus he argues that even if any of us were miracle workers and had all kinds of spiritual gifts, without love we are nothing. The word Paul uses for love ('αγάπη) (agape) is not the kind of love that seeks some kind of reward from the one we love (i.e., it is not based on what we can get out of a relationship). Agape is a giving kind of love, the kind of love that Jesus has for us. St. John tells us: "God is love (agape)," (1 John 4:8) so if we're without love we're without God and vice versa. Without being connected with God, we're not connected to the head or to the rest of the body.

Our Mass helps us to abide in his love. We listen to his words, we recall his sacrifice on the cross for us, and we are united with him, the source of all love (agape), in Communion. We ask his help though our prayers and we give thanks for his love for us. Don't forget ευχαριστία (eucharistia) is the Greek word for giving thanks and that's what we are doing now.

## 5th Sunday in Ordinary Time
### February 7, 2010

**INTRODUCTION** – (Isaiah 6:1-2a, 3-8; 1 Corinthians 15:1-11; Luke 5:1-11) Our first reading is one of my favorite Old Testament readings. It is from the prophet Isaiah who lived about 725 years before Christ. He describes his call from God to be a prophet. The setting is in Jerusalem in the Temple. Notice he is unable to describe what God looks like. He describes God's royal robe, the angels, the sounds and the profound sense of God's holiness. In this experience he becomes aware of his own unworthiness. You will recognize in this passage the inspiration for two familiar hymns: the Holy, Holy, which we say or sing at every Mass and the hymn, Here I Am, Lord.

In the other two readings we hear how two other people experienced God in Jesus Christ: Paul in his vision of the Risen Christ and Peter in the miraculous catch of fish.

**HOMILY** – Several years ago, Rabbi Joseph Telushkin wrote a little book called *Jewish Humor: What the Best Jewish Jokes Say about the Jews.* In it he tells this story: A man takes some very fine material to a tailor and asks the tailor to make him a pair of pants. He goes back a week later, but the pants are not ready. Two weeks go by, and still the pants are not ready. Finally, after six weeks, the pants are ready. The man tries them, and they fit perfectly. As he pays for them, he says to the tailor, "It took God only six days to make the world. And it took you six weeks to make just one pair of pants." "Yes," said the tailor, "but look at the pair of pants (perfect!) and look at the world (it's a mess)." The tailor was hinting that perhaps God would have done a better job if he weren't in so much of a hurry.

I wonder if the tailor ever read his bible. It tells us from the very beginning all that God made was good. God, moreover, put his human creatures in the garden of Eden, a paradise that would be a source of every delight. But God's first human creatures rebelled against God and destroyed the harmony and joy God had blessed them with. Somehow we, the children of those first humans, continue to follow their example. So if the world is in a mess, the bible is telling us, don't blame God. We humans have created that mess ourselves.

Maybe God really didn't create the world in six days. After all the bible is not trying to teach science. It's trying to tell us that God made all things, not how. You may have heard the story that after God made Adam, and Adam was in the Garden of Eden for a while, God asked Adam how things were going. Adam told God he was enjoying everything, but he felt something was missing. God said, how about if I create a companion for you, someone you can put your arms around, someone who will laugh at your jokes, listen to your stories, who will give you no hassle and will cater to your every whim. Adam thought that would be great. God said it will cost you an arm and a leg. Adam thought for a few moments, then asked God, what can I get for a rib.

We know there is a lot of symbolism in the two creation accounts of Genesis. For example, men are not going around with a rib missing. The six days of creation is also symbolic. Scholars tell us this account of creation was written by a priest who was trying to teach his people, among other things, that they were to keep holy the Sabbath. Even God rested on the Sabbath. Actually God doesn't get tired and his work of creation is ongoing. Astronomy has discovered that new stars are forming all the time. New human beings are coming into the world all the time. Even Jesus told the Jewish leaders after one of his miracles: "My father is at work until now, so I am at work." (Jn 5:7). We heard how God is at work making the world better through his prophet, Isaiah. God appeared to Isaiah, and purified his lips so that he could proclaim God's message to God's people. God was at work through St. Paul in today's second reading proclaiming the resurrection. I would like to expand on this passage a little more. Paul's letter is one of the earliest writings in the New Testament, written about the year 56 or 57 (about 14 years before the first gospel was written), thus it is a very important testimony to the faith of the early Church. The Corinthians were having a problem accepting the idea of the resurrection of the body. They thought our body came back to life with the same problems, weaknesses, and flaws it had before we died. They thought their spirits would be freer without their bodies. That's not so, Paul said. He tells them "what I handed on to you, as of first importance, I also received." Because it is such an important doctrine, Paul dedicated the whole last part of his letter to the resurrection. Notice the kind of language he uses to indicate this is the Tradition of the Church: "I handed on to you what I also received." That is, this is what the

Church always believed about Jesus, that although he was put to death, his body now lives and he is seated at the right hand of God the Father. Paul goes on (beyond today's passage) to explain how we too shall rise to new life with him. It is a new world God is creating, in the risen Lord Jesus. That's where our gospel comes in: Peter and the apostles, who were among the many who visibly saw Jesus after his resurrection, would now be catching people, Jesus told Peter. They would be bringing people into God's perfect Kingdom, leading them though baptism and the Eucharist to a new life, eternal life, where there would be no more pain or suffering or even death.

When we look around and see that the world is in terrible shape, let us not lose hope. God hasn't abandoned us, rather God continues to send people who will help to establish his eternal Kingdom, people like Isaiah, people like Paul, people like Peter and the apostles, people like you and me. Amen.

## 6th Sunday in Ordinary Time
### February 14, 2010

**INTRODUCTION** – (Jeremiah 17:5-8; 1 Cor. 15:12, 16-20; Lk. 6:17, 20-26) Today we hear from the prophet Jeremiah. He lived during the final years before the Babylonians destroyed the land of Judah, Jerusalem, the Temple, and took most of its citizens off as captives and slaves to Babylon. If you read Jeremiah, you will see how God constantly called God's people back to fidelity to their Jewish faith and how they always turned their back on God and relied on their own human resources. Today we hear part of one of Jeremiah's homilies where he reminds God's people that their only hope of survival was in God. Jeremiah was ignored, hated, punished, and almost put to death for preaching God's Word, but he could not stop for he was totally committed to God's work and he found strength in God's power.

HOMILY – On this Valentine's Day I would like to offer a couple of stories about loving spouses. The first is about a woman whose van was buried in the family driveway. Her husband came to her rescue, digging her out, rocking the van and pushing her free. As she was driving down the road she heard an unusual noise. She got on her cell phone and called home. When her husband answered the phone she said: "Thank God you answered, there was some horrible sound coming from under the van. For a moment I thought I was dragging you down the highway." "And you didn't stop?" he asked. I'm sure in his love he gave her a valentine anyway.

The second takes place in a church where the people offer spontaneous intentions at the intercession time. One man, Bob, asked for prayers for himself and his wife on their 37th anniversary. At the obvious nudging of his wife he corrected that to 38th anniversary. As the chuckling died down, heard from the back of church was, "I'd like to offer a prayer for Bob." (both stories are from *Reader's Digest, Laughter the Best Medicine* – pg 153)

St. Valentine, the patron saint of lovers, was a Roman priest, physician and martyr who was put to death sometime around 270 A.D. A basilica was built on the spot where he was buried some years later after the emperor Constantine made Christianity the official religion of the empire. The custom of sending a "Valentine" to a loved one stems from the medieval belief that birds choose their mates on this day. It's unfortunate we need reminders to tell those we love that we love them. I always encourage married couples to tell one another that they love each other.

Jeremiah is telling us there are only two ways to live our lives: trusting in God and faithfully following him or trying to make our own way through life while ignoring the direction and the grace God gives us. The reading from Jeremiah, telling us how to find true happiness in life, prepared the way for the gospel where Jesus preaches the beatitudes. Beatitude is a word that means blessed or happy. Luke and Matthew have two different versions of the beatitudes. In Luke we hear four beatitudes and four conditions that begin with the word "woe," an expression denoting pain or displeasure, hardship or distress. Matthew has eight beatitudes. Luke is speaking to a distinct audience who in fact were poor, hungry and downcast at times, under the oppression of a foreign power. Some of those who were the oppressors were the ones who were exploiting the poor and having a good time at their expense. Matthew has Jesus speaking to a more general audience when he said "Blessed are the poor in spirit" Neither is saying that being poor is a blessing and having wealth is evil. Some of Jesus' friends were wealthy, at least by the standards of the time. In both Matthew and Luke, Jesus is telling us through the beatitudes there will come a time when things will be reversed for the poor, the sorrowing, the hungry, the oppressed. In both gospels the beatitudes look forward to a blessedness that is to come, which begins here and now for all who follow Christ faithfully.

This is what St. Paul is telling us in the second reading. The Corinthians had difficulty believing in the resurrection. But Paul tells them our whole faith, our whole salvation, our whole Christian way of life begins and is founded on the resurrection of Jesus. Not only that but we who have followed Christ will share in his resurrection. Jesus was the first fruits, that is, the first indication of what God has planned for all who love him and serve him. At Mass we commemorate his death and resurrection which promise us new life. Amen.

## 1st Sunday of Lent
### February 21, 2010

**INTRODUCTION** – (Deut. 26:4-10; Rom. 10:8-13; Lk.4:1-13) In our first reading from Deuteronomy, we hear Moses instructing the people in the proper way to offer God thanks and praise for their freedom and for the land God had given them. In gratitude for their blessings, they were to offer their tithes to the Lord – one tenth of the fruits of their land. Along with their offering they would profess they were once a people without freedom or land, and they would now bring their offering in gratitude for all the ways God had blessed them. The reading prepares us for the gospel where Satan tries to tempt Jesus into worshipping him so as to gain power over all earthly kingdoms. Jesus' answer comes from another part of the book of Deuteronomy which says, "You shall worship the Lord your God and him alone shall you serve." (Deut. 6:13)

**HOMILY** – You may have heard this story before. A man named Paddy (which is short for Patrick) came from Ireland to Boston. In a very short time, he began the practice of going to the local bar after work and ordering three beers. He wanted them served to him all at once. After a few weeks the bartender asked Paddy why he insisted having all three beers served at the same time. He explained that when he lived in Ireland, he and his two brothers always got together after work for a beer. He wanted to keep the spirit of their getting together even though they still lived across the sea. A few months went by and one day Paddy came in and ordered just two beers. The bartender was concerned and asked if something happened to one of his brothers. Paddy said "No, it's nothing like that. You see it's Lent now and I've given up beer for Lent."

Every year on the first Sunday of Lent, we hear about Jesus going into the wilderness for 40 days to fast and pray. This gospel is meant to inspire us to make these next 40 days a spiritual preparation for Easter through prayer and sacrifice. Paddy had the idea that this is a time of sacrifice, but he wasn't going to overdo it!

There are an infinite number of things we can do to make these days special. Our goal can be to give up something such as actions or habits or attitudes that get in our way as we try to love God and others, or our goal can be positive as we try to do things that can help us grow in our love for God and for others.

Notice at the beginning of our gospel reading today, St. Luke tells us Jesus was filled with the Holy Spirit. Jesus had just been baptized in the Jordan by John the Baptist and the Holy Spirit had descended upon him. But that didn't prevent the devil from showing up. Everyone is tested by temptation and sometimes we're tested the most right after we make a decision to be a better person and to love and serve God more faithfully. Temptation doesn't necessarily come from the devil; the world and the flesh provide enough temptation in our lives too. No one is so holy that they will not be tempted. Luke's gospel tells us at the end the devil departed from him "for a time." The devil doesn't rest as St. Peter tells us.

I would like to briefly comment on Jesus' three temptations. 1) Jesus' first temptation was to use his uniquely miraculous power for his own benefit: "turn these stones into bread." But Jesus came to serve and he reserved his special power to help others. 2) The devil then told Jesus all earthly kingdoms belonged to him and he would turn them over to Jesus if Jesus would worship him. The devil is noted for telling big lies. Jesus called the devil the "father of lies" in John's gospel (Jn. 8:44) and he did not fall for the devil's deception. 3) Then the devil took Jesus to the top of the Temple and told him to jump for nothing would happen to him if he were the Son of God. In Matthew's gospel this is the second temptation; however, Luke makes it the third, probably because the Temple is so important in the structure of Luke's gospel. If those who were in the Temple area were to see Jesus slowly descending from above, they would immediately acclaim him as messiah for that's the way many people expected the messiah to arrive. It would be an easy way for Jesus to get a following, but it was not ease and popularity Jesus sought. His was to do the Father's will, which would involve fidelity to his mission of teaching, a mission that would gain him many enemies and a fidelity that would lead to his suffering and death.

Our forty days have just begun. Whatever prayer or sacrifice or good work we may have determined to do during this sacred time, I would bet that one temptation all of us will have (at least I always do) is to say to ourselves "40 days is too long." Don't give up whatever your good works might happen to be. Our works and prayers will be a source of blessings for each of us and for all of us. Amen.

# 2nd Sunday of Lent
## February 28, 2010

**INTRODUCTION** – (Gen. 15:5-12, 17-18; Phil, 3:20-4:1; Luke 9:28b-36) Abram, whose name was later changed to Abraham, lived almost 4000 years ago. God had already inspired him to leave his home in southern Iraq (Ur of the Caldeans) and make a new home in the Land of Canaan. Today we hear God make two promises to Abram 1) he would have so many descendants they could not be counted and 2) someday his descendants would occupy the entire land of Canaan. As a proof that these promises would ever be fulfilled, God gave Abram a sign which consisted of a covenant ritual, a common practice in those days. This ritual involved those who were making the covenant to cut an animal in half and then walking between the halves. It was a symbolic way of saying, "may the same thing happen to me as to this animal if I am unfaithful to my promise." God is often represented as light and/or fire in the Scriptures. In this experience only God, symbolized as fire and light, moved between the two halves of the animals. This indicated that God was not asking anything in return from Abram except for his trust, a trust that would be tested in many ways, but a trust that Abram always maintained. In the psalm that follows, we express our own trust in God as our light and our salvation."

**HOMILY** – I have four important topics I want to touch on today. (1) We'll begin with the gospel. The gospels try to get us to answer for ourselves a very important question. The question is the one Jesus asked his disciples at Caesarea Philippi: "Who do you say that I am?" We all know Peter's answer: "You are the Messiah." His answer is a partial answer to the question of who Jesus is, and Jesus complimented Peter for it. He also clearly told Peter that Peter still had so much more he needed to understand. Today's gospel gives us another piece of the answer. All three gospels closely connect the transfiguration of Jesus to Peter's profession of faith. They seldom pay much attention to issues of time, but they all make a point that it was about a week later that Jesus took Peter, James and John up a high mountain and the divine glory radiated from him. The voice from the cloud helps us further to answer the question, "Who do you say that I am?" God said: "This is my Son, my Chosen One. Listen to him." They say a picture is worth a thousand words, so I would like to show you four pictures: First is Mt. Tabor. The gospels do not tell us this is the place where the transfiguration took place, but it is the traditional site. It stands out all by itself in the middle of the plain of Jezreel. This next picture is a closer picture with the road going to the top. When I was in Israel several years ago, a bus took us only part way up, then a taxi had to finish taking us to the top because buses couldn't make those turns. I had the privilege of being the main presider at the Mass our group celebrated when we got to the church at the top. This third picture is a painting by Giovanni Bellini. It's not quite so dramatic as the one by Raphael. Raphael showed us what was going on at the base of the mountain while Jesus was being transfigured. The apostles were trying to cast a demon out of a young boy and they couldn't because their faith wasn't strong enough. They all had to wait until Jesus returned so he could cast it out. Our best lesson from the transfiguration is, I think, the words of God the Father: "This is my Beloved Son, my Chosen One; listen to him." He is worth listening to for he will bring us into eternal glory as St. Paul tells us.

(2) My second item today: I want to thank all of our parishioners and visitors for their great response to my

October appeal for increased donations. Back in October when I made my appeal, we were about $6000 in the red. Today we are about $15,000 to the good. But I hasten to say: please don't ease up, because other sources of revenue such as bequests and special gifts are lagging behind and besides, in fiscal year 08-09 we lost $59,000. It is important to say "thank you," so I am mentioning this so I can say "thank you very much."

(3) I want to let you know from me personally, and not second hand, that we are making some changes in the administration of our school. Sister Ann knows she has reached her limit and she is no longer able to keep up as she has done so well in the past. I know that if I had to keep a schedule as she does, they would have buried me ten years ago. As I see it, she had three options: 1) to just hang on, wearing herself out and not being able to do as good a job as she needed to do, 2) to hand in her resignation and say goodbye and good luck, or 3) to continue working in a reduced capacity as co-principal. Sister would continue to be involved helping children with special needs, doing PR, development and giving input and help to a new principal. On top of this, the Mercy Sisters will be subsidizing Sr. Ann's salary. In other words, we're keeping her expertise and involvement in the school without any cost at all. To me that was a no-brainer. The idea was Sister Ann's idea and I am delighted that she will remain involved in the school. We chose Jason Fightmaster, who has been a teacher as well as our acting vice-principal for the past several years, to be co-principal with her. He will carry the burden of the day to day operation of the school. We will have to hire a teacher to take over his teaching position and we will have to pay him more as principal. This third option will cost us an extra $20,000 next year, but I think it would be less expensive overall than either

of the other two options.

Number four, the Catholic Ministry Appeal will begin this week and, of course, we need your help. This appeal is exclusively for six Archdiocesan ministries. Two-thirds of your donation will go toward the education of priests and ministers at the Athenaeum, Catholic Charities and Social Services, and retired diocesan priests. Thus Fr. Lammeier benefits from this collection and some day I hope to be able to. The other third will go for College Campus Ministries, chaplains for hospitals and prisons, and St. Rita's School for the Deaf. Nothing is used for Archdiocesan administration. All these worthwhile causes are related to ministries that would be beyond the capability of any single parish to maintain. We have gone over our goal every year for the past 18 years. So I am very hopeful that our parish can meet our goal of $16,100, which is only $300 more than last year. Whatever you can give will be greatly appreciated, even if it's $10. Last year I suggested that if everyone who could pledge or donate $100 did so, we would make our goal. I would make the same suggestion this year. You will receive a letter from Archbishop Schnurr this week with a pledge card and donation envelope. Please bring your pledge or donation with you next week and put it in the collection basket.

Those are all the items I want to talk about today. I hope perhaps you have a greater appreciation of Jesus' transfiguration. As we gather together with our Lord today, I hope you might feel as the apostles did: "Lord, it is good that we are here."

# 3rd Sunday of Lent
## March 7, 2010

**INTRODUCTION** – (Exodus 3:1-8a, 13-15; 1 Corinthians 10:1-6,10-12; Luke 13:1-9) Our psalm refrain, "The Lord is kind and merciful," describes our theme for today. We hear about God's desire to bring his people, suffering as slaves in Egypt, into freedom. He chooses Moses to be the one to demand and obtain their freedom. Moses wasn't happy to have to do this. He had escaped from Egypt himself because he had killed an Egyptian who had attacked an Israelite. Now God tells him he has to go back and deal with the Egyptian king. God gives Moses a special gift, God's name: "Yahweh," translated as "I AM." What is so special about that? It was like giving someone your private phone number. God was assuring Moses of a special relationship Moses would have with him and letting Moses know he could call on God whenever he needed him.

In our second reading Paul reminds us of how many blessings and marvels God's people experienced as God led them through the desert to the Promised Land. But in spite of all the wonderful things God gave them, they were unable to enter into the Promised Land. In the end they had failed to continue trusting in God. He tells us not to be like them.

The theme that "the Lord is kind and merciful" shows up again in the gospel in a short parable about a fig tree. It was given opportunities of every kind to produce fruit, but it failed to do so. "The Lord is kind and merciful," but he expects us not to take his mercy for granted. With the help of his kindness, he expects us to grow in goodness and holiness.

**HOMILY** – A young girl brought her boyfriend home

to meet her parents. The parents couldn't find many good qualities about him. When the parents had the opportunity to talk to their daughter later, by herself, the girl's mother said: "Dear, he doesn't seem like a very nice person." "Mom," the daughter answered, "if he wasn't nice, why would he be doing 500 hours of community service?"

It's stretching things a bit to say "community service" fits into the theme of today's liturgy, but our readings remind us not to be like the fig tree in Jesus' parable today. We are to produce good works. God didn't create us just to take up space in this world. He wants more from us than that. He wants us to trust him, to love him and to do good for others.

I said in my introduction that the theme for today is "the Lord is kind and merciful." He is kind and merciful in many ways. One of the ways he is kind and merciful is in calling us to repentance and renewal. In the book of Revelation Jesus said: "Whoever is dear to me I reprove and chastise. Be earnest about it, therefore. Repent! Here I stand, knocking at the door. If anyone hears me calling and opens the door, I will enter his house and have supper with him, and he with me." This assumes that we all have room for improvement. God asks that of us and he also gives us the help we need to be better. That is kindness to us. He would not be kind if he didn't stimulate us to keep improving ourselves. The fact that he challenges us to change comes from his love as a caring parent. The parable of the fig tree is a call to live a positive life according to the gospel – doing good by loving God and others.

The conversation Jesus had about tragic events at the beginning of today's gospel was interesting. Sometimes people think when something bad happens to someone it is God's punishment. Jesus said that's not always true.

He does not try to explain suffering here, but he is telling us not to be complacent, which we sometimes are. We can't think "well, if nothing bad is happening to me, it must be because I am so good." He tells us we <u>all</u> need to repent, i.e., to work to be better than we are.

This season of Lent keeps reminding us of our need to grow in holiness and goodness. Many people I have talked with do nothing special during Lent. They think they're good enough. Others start off Lent with a great deal of enthusiasm praying more, making sacrifices or doing good work. But as the weeks drag on, they ease up with their good resolutions. We still have four more weeks of Lent. Our readings today are encouraging us to do what we can so we can come to Easter with mind and heart renewed.

Today we have the first of three Scrutinies. Our community prays for those who are preparing to come into the Church at Easter so that they are better able to live the Christian way of life. May we all do a better job of living up to what God wants of us. We must remember, though, at all times, whether God is comforting us, forgiving us, healing us, blessing us, encouraging us or correcting us, "The Lord is kind and merciful."

# 4th Sunday of Lent
## March 14, 2010

HOMILY – (Joshua 5:9a, 10-12; 2 Corinthians 5:17-21; Luke 15:1-3, 11-32) We just heard the story of a young boy whose life was misdirected by love of riches and pleasure. After his so called friends abandoned him and he suffered hunger and want for a period of time, he came to his senses and returned to his father. He returned a changed person. Fortunately, he had a loving and forgiving father who accepted him unconditionally. The point of the story is abundantly clear when we consider the relationship between the father and his younger son. As regards the relationship between the father and the older son, Jesus leaves the conclusion open-ended. We have to reflect on what might have happened, whether the older son gave in to his father's pleading to be forgiving or whether he refused. How we end the story will tell us a lot about ourselves.

I want to tell you about another young man whose story is somewhat similar. He was Catholic to start with but admits that he was not a very good one. His father was a government official and this young man enjoyed the comforts of those who were well off. He described himself at sixteen as a scatterbrained youth who had "turned away from God and did not keep his commandments." As his story goes, he was kidnapped and sold as a slave and made to labor on a farm for six years. Like the prodigal son who was without friends and who suffered without adequate food or shelter, this young man came to his senses and he learned obedience through what he suffered. He discovered (and we quote) "God showed me how to have faith in him forever, as one who is never to be doubted." After six years God spoke to him in a way that he heard with his own ears. He would escape and God audibly told him when to leave and what direction to go in order to accomplish his escape. Miraculously God protected him along the way until he arrived back home. Like the prodigal son, he came home a new person. Although his parents wanted to keep him at home with them, his love for God led him to want to serve God as a priest. Even more than serving as a priest, his love for others led him to want to return to the people who captured and enslaved him and teach them about God. And that he did. After overcoming many obstacles, including rejection by the hierarchy, a breach of confidence by a friend to whom he entrusted a confession of his past life, his lack of education and social graces, he returned as a bishop to the people who had enslaved him. Once he arrived he wasn't greeted with open arms. Again, in his own words, he said "daily I expect either murder, or robbery, or enslavement." He writes elsewhere "they seized me with my companions. And on that day they most eagerly desired to kill me; but my time had not yet come. And everything they found with us they plundered, and myself they bound in chains." He feared nothing, for even if he were to be put to death, he felt that would have been the supreme act of love for his God. But God had other intentions than that he should be a martyr. For 30 years he served God and the people who once enslaved him and his work was blessed. He ordained many bishops and priests, established convents, monasteries and schools and in thirty years saw the conversion of almost all of Ireland. And of course you all know I've been talking about St. Patrick, who is one of our patronal saints and whose statue is under the choir loft. His work was so successful that in a short time Ireland was sending out missionaries to revitalize the faith of Europe which had fallen into decline. Irish missionaries have been a blessing to the Church ever since.

For those who are Irish and who honor Patrick, the best way to truly honor him is not by drinking a Guinness. We should respond to his example and his call to holiness. Again quoting Patrick, he asks those who believe in him and love him to "strengthen and confirm your faith...That will be my glory, for a wise son is the glory of his father."

And for those who are not Irish and who think too much is made of St. Patrick on March 17th, I would like you to think of how our faith has been strengthened by the witness of many Irish saints and how our civilization has been preserved by the scholarship of the Irish during the days when mainland Europe was being overrun by barbarians. The great heritage of western civilization, from the Greek and Roman classics to Jewish and Christian works, would have been utterly lost were it not for the holy men and women of unconquered Ireland. These Irish recorded the great works of western civilization in their monasteries and convents (remember all books had to be written by hand). They brought this learning back to Europe after it began to stabilize in the eighth century under Charlemagne. Whether you're Irish or not, we all owe a great debt to the Irish and we pray that our patron, St. Patrick, blesses our parish and our families.

## 5th Sunday of Lent
### March 21, 2010

**INTRODUCTION** – (Isaiah 43:6-21; Philippians 3:8-14; John 8:1-11) God's people were a captive people, enslaved by the Babylonians 600 years before Christ. After 50 years of captivity, God sent them a prophet to announce to them that they were about to be set free. We hear that prophet in today's first reading. God tells them their release from the Babylonians would be no less spectacular than their release from slavery in Egypt centuries earlier. Even as the prophet speaks, he tells them the road back to their own land is being made ready. God's statement, "see, I am doing something new" leads us into the gospel. There we hear about a woman caught in adultery who was about to be sentenced to death. Jesus is doing something new: offering forgiveness rather than condemnation.

**HOMILY** – One afternoon the parish priest was getting ready to hear confessions. As he entered the confessional room, which had a divider in it, he found a man already in the room waiting for him. The man told the parish priest, "It's been 45 years since I've been to confession. I am impressed how things have changed. The room is well lit, it's a nice easy chair to sit in, a bottle of scotch, some nice cigars. It wasn't that way the last time I went." The parish priest said, "yes, it is rather comfortable, but where you are sitting is my side of the confessional room." By the way, if anyone wants to check out our confessional, they are welcome to. It's pretty simple.

I thought I might say something about confession today. The sacrament referred to as "confession" is also called the sacrament of penance or reconciliation. I thought the topic might be appropriate because of today's gospel where Jesus, as he had done many times in the gospels, demonstrates God's merciful love.

He did not come to condemn but to save. In the old days, which many of us remember, the priest often thought his job was to scold the penitent. Many people never came back because of that. I always tell our people in the RCIA, if a priest starts to bawl you out, get up and leave. Go to someone else who sees their role as that of Christ who offers freedom from guilt and shame and a sense of God's peace. Fortunately, I was blest with that kind of a confessor almost all my life. I've always felt that scolding doesn't help them to grow spiritually, but offering a person the chance to start over and the opportunity to know God's love does help a person to grow. Imagine how this woman in the gospel was changed by her encounter with Christ.

Jesus came not to condemn but to save. And that's the purpose of confession or reconciliation. Sometimes the priest tries to guide a person to see how wrong their behavior might be, but that guidance should be done in a gentle and loving way. The only time I know that Jesus was ever harsh with anyone was with the religious leaders who thought they were perfect and refused to see their faults. We're all sinners. We are all in need of God's mercy and love. That's why Christ came to us. You'll notice when the chips were down and Jesus started writing on the ground, no one threw any stones. They knew he had called their bluff. Some people have speculated that Jesus was writing people's sins, but no one knows for sure. Anyway, we're all in the same boat with the crowd in the gospel, we would all have to walk away if Jesus said, "let the one among you who is without sin cast the first stone at her." Jesus does not whitewash sin or ignore the seriousness of it. More than anyone he knows how it hurts us and hurts our relationship with God. Notice he told the woman, "go and from now on, do not sin any more." The old catechism called this "a firm purpose of amendment."

In the first five or six centuries of the Church, people were allowed to receive confession only once in their lifetime. It was only for publicly committed serious sins. The attitude of Church leaders was that if a person sinned again, there was no hope for them. In addition, people had to go through a period of public penance before reconciliation. In around the sixth or seventh century, mostly due to the influence of the monasteries, a practice developed where the sacrament began to be used as spiritual direction. People went, even though they had no grave sins, and they went more frequently. It is the practice we have today, although many more people took advantage of the sacrament two or three generations ago than they do now. I think a person should go at least once or twice a year just to help themselves grow spiritually.

The sacrament of reconciliation is one of the most rewarding parts of being a priest, especially when I know I have helped lift a burden of guilt and self-hatred off a person's conscience. I am blest to be able to participate in the process of bringing God's love and peace to someone. I might mention that we have our penance service this Wednesday. There is an insert in today's bulletin describing how to make a good confession. Amen.

# Passion Sunday
## March 28, 2010

(*Gospel: blessing of palms: Luke 19:28-40*) I showed on a screen in church the 1820 painting by Benjamin Haydon. It hangs in our seminary in Mt. Washington, the Athenaeum. It is one of the most famous works of Haydon. We were told when we were in the seminary that Haydon painted the face of Jesus several times until he was satisfied. I personally think he was attempting to portray the divinity shining from Jesus.

Our mood changes now from one of praise and celebration to one that is very serious as we hear in our readings what Jesus would have to suffer in order to fulfill his mission as savior and messiah.

**HOMILY** – (*readings at Mass: Isaiah 50:4-7; Philippians 2:6-11; Luke 22:14-23, 56*) Jesus entered Jerusalem riding on a donkey. To us that doesn't seem so dignified, but that's the way most people traveled in those days – unless they walked. Horses were generally used for war. Even the kings in Israel and Judea, who lived before Jesus, rode on a donkey and that is how Jesus entered

Jerusalem – as the long awaited king of Israel (a.k.a "the messiah"). Since there probably wasn't a red carpet nearby, the people spread branches and cloaks making the rutted and miry road a little smoother. In Matthew and Mark the people call him Son of David, thus indicating he is a member of the royal family of King David and they shout Hosanna which literally means "save us." They wanted to have their own king who could save them from the oppressive power of the Romans (which they hated). St. Luke, whose gospel we heard, has the people proclaim: "Blessed is the king who comes in the name of the Lord."

Jerusalem would have been filled with Jews since Passover was about to be celebrated. Thus Jews would have vastly outnumbered the Roman soldiers who were stationed in the city. If there were ever to be a revolt against Rome, this would have been the time to make it happen. So this triumphal entry, to the shouts of "Hosanna" (save us), and "Son of David" who comes as "king in the name of the Lord" would have made the Romans very, very nervous. The Jewish religious leaders were very troubled too, for Jesus was a major challenge to their authority and, although they looked forward to the Messiah, Jesus wasn't the Messiah they wanted.

Those who felt threatened by him, especially the Jewish religious leaders, looked for a chance to get him, and they did. They put him on trial and worked hard to find a charge against him. The only offense they could pin on him in order to bring him before Pilate, the Roman governor and the only one who had power to put him to death, was to accuse Jesus of claiming to be their king. And he didn't deny it. All he had to do was deny it. The trial would have been over and he would have been a free man. But he could not deny who he was. In Mark's gospel, Jesus answers clearly that he is king of the

Jews, but here in Luke Jesus answers indirectly: "You say that I am" or "You say so." His answer is not so direct and we wonder why. Could it be that in answering the way he did, he is making every person throughout all of history come to their own conclusion as to who he is. We all have to answer for ourselves this most important question he asked the disciples at Caesarea Philippi: "Who do *you* say that I am?"

We know how Pilate answered that question. He had "Jesus Christ, king of the Jews" written in Hebrew, Latin and Greek attached to the cross above Jesus' head. But he didn't mean it. He just did that as a slap in the face for the Jews.

As we answer that question, are we with Pilate who is willing to call Jesus king, but not really mean it. Are we the Jewish leaders who judged him to be an impostor. Are we with the crowd who acclaimed him as king and messiah when it was the popular thing to do but who later deserted him. Are we with his disciples who were looking for someone to rescue them from oppression and suffering. Or are we with those few faithful disciples who were willing to follow him even to Calvary?

This week gives us a lot of opportunity to reflect on who Jesus is and especially who he is for *us*. Amen.

# Holy Thursday
## April 9, 2009

HOMILY – (Exodus 12:1-8, 11-14; 1 Cor 11:23-26; John 13:1-15) Fran told me two weeks ago this is the time of the year when people hang up on her when she calls. That's because for years Fran has been so kind as to recruit people for the foot washing. A lot of people avoid talking to her as we get closer to Holy Thursday. People react like Peter: "Fr. Joe will never wash my feet." Well, I'll admit it is humbling to have your pastor kneel in front of you and wash your feet. For me, though, it's not very humbling at all. I think it's very special. But in Jesus' day it was a different story. It was a dirty job. People in those days didn't wear shoes and socks. They wore something more like sandals, and most people walked when they went anywhere. They walked the same dusty, dirty roads that herds of animals walked on. So you can imagine people's feet were dirty and smelly. Having their feet washed when they went to someone's house for dinner would have been refreshing. But the master of the house didn't do the foot washing. Slaves or servants did that job and where there were no slaves or servants, the children or the wife did it. I suppose if I wanted to be really humble, I would go wash the feet of several homeless people and have no audience or pretty singing while I was doing it. But we do it tonight to dramatize what Jesus did.

One of our candidates for foot washing remarked, "I don't know what to think about this." Well, Jesus did a lot of teaching and a lot of healing and helping people. But this last night with his apostles before his death, he wanted to really do something off the wall that would stick with them and symbolize what he was all about. So he told them how to think about what he had done. He said: "I have given you a model to follow, so that as I have done for you, you should also do." He had previously told us, "Whoever wishes to be great among you must be your servant, and whoever wishes to be first among you must be your slave." He gave us an example of the great commandment of love; that we should love one another as he has loved us.

But there was an interesting interchange between Jesus and Peter. When Jesus came to Peter, Peter basically asked, "why are you going to wash my feet?" Jesus said, "you don't understand now why I'm doing it, you will understand later." Peter protested, "you will never wash my feet." Jesus said (and I like this translation better), "If I do not wash you, you won't belong to me." That is as strong a statement as Jesus could have made. I asked myself why Jesus was so definite and why it was so important that everyone have their feet washed, even Peter? Thinking of what Jesus was doing as a demonstration of service, it struck me that we all need to allow ourselves to let Jesus serve us. In what ways does he serve us? He serves us through his sacrificial death on the cross and his resurrection. In his words, he came to seek out and to save the one who is lost; and that's all of us. It's only when we know we need to be saved that we will really know Jesus for that's what the name "Jesus" means: God saves. How do we make this connection with his saving love? Two ways: prayer and the sacraments. In those two ways Jesus can serve us and save us.

Especially in the Eucharist does Jesus come to us to bring us the love and life he wants to share with us. He makes himself vulnerable to us. We can receive him with love, we can receive him with indifference, we can receive him with distraction, we can be too busy to bother coming to receive him at all. But for those who open the door of their heart to him, he is there to share a meal with us as friends. (Rev. 3:20) What greater gift can he give us than himself. "My flesh is real food and my blood real drink," he tells us in John's sixth chapter on the Eucharist.

Tonight we recall Jesus' last supper with his disciples. He came to serve them and he did serve them as their teacher and Lord, but now he was about to serve them (and all of us) by his death on a cross. He demonstrated to us how we are to serve one another and gave us a command to do so. And at the Last Supper he gave us a way to remember what he has done for us and how he continues to bring us into union with his saving work, the Eucharist. "Do this in memory of me" we hear him say twice in tonight's second reading, the oldest recorded account of the institution of the Eucharist.

We may not understand it all, we may not understand why Jesus had to die to save us, we may not understand how a small host and a sip of wine can bring Jesus to us, we may not even understand why God would love us so much as to send his Son to save us, but as Jesus said to Peter: "you will understand later." Amen.

# Good Friday
## April 2, 2010

**HOMILY** – (Is 52:13-53:12; Heb 4:14-16, 5:7-9; John 18:1-19:42) Every day we gather around this altar to celebrate the Eucharist. In the Eucharist God's love is shown to us through Jesus Christ who gave his life for us on the cross. So he can share his life with us now, he continues to give us his body and blood. The gift of his life involved immense suffering on his part. Our gospels do not dwell long on his sufferings. They didn't need to because the people who lived at the time the gospels were written knew what crucifixion involved. It was one of the most agonizing forms of execution that human beings had ever concocted. On this one day of the year, out of respect for what Jesus went through, we do not celebrate the Eucharist as we do every other day. Instead we have a rather extended service of reflection, intercessions, and Communion.

Rather than focusing on the physical sufferings of Jesus, I would like to reflect on the mystery of suffering itself. The book of Genesis attributes suffering to sin. The first man and woman God created lost the happiness God had intended for them because of their disobedience to God. The whole first part of the Old Testament, Deuteronomy, Judges, Samuel and Kings and many of the prophets reflects this notion of suffering – that it is caused by disobedience to God. There is some truth in that notion, but it is not the whole story as the Book of Job tells us. Without telling us why good people suffer, the Book of Job took issue with the old theology on suffering. Sometime about 500 years before Christ, the prophet Isaiah gave us a new way of thinking about suffering – that it can have a positive purpose – that one person's suffering can bring blessings to another. We heard it clearly expressed in today's first reading from a passage in Isaiah known as the 4th Servant Song. I would like to repeat some phrases from our first reading; they are so powerful. God's Servant, Isaiah says, "was spurned and avoided by people, a man of suffering, accustomed to infirmity…Yet it was our infirmities that he bore, our sufferings that he endured…he was pierced for our offenses, crushed for our sins; upon him was the chastisement that makes us whole, by his stripes we were healed…though he had done no wrong nor spoken any falsehood, the Lord was pleased to crush him in infirmity… he shall take away the sins of many and win pardon for their offenses."

It is easy to see in a family how one person's sufferings can benefit another person. For example, how parents make sacrifices for their children, how they have to go through difficult times to support those they love and teach them and discipline them. The sufferings of Jesus, however, were a scandal to his followers. The Messiah was not expected to suffer. We remember when Jesus tried to warn his disciples that he would "suffer greatly and be killed and would rise again." Peter replied, "Heaven forbid, Lord, this will never happen to you." Jesus response to Peter is familiar to all of us: "Get behind me, Satan."

Why did he have to suffer? I have asked myself that question many times and others have asked me that question many times as well. My current thinking on this is I think he had to suffer because of who he was. He was God's Son who came among a sinful people. He could not be anything other than who he was and, without redemption, we could not be anything other than who we are. He was like a lamb dropped into a tigers' cage. He was from above, we are from this world, his holiness did not fit in with our sinful ways. The only kingdom we could know was the kingdom of this world and his kingdom did not belong to this world. Thus he came to his own and his own received him not. Because he could not be other than who he was and because he was faithful to the purpose for which he came – his purpose being to confront the powers of evil, to heal and to teach us to change our lives and to live in a new way – conflict, confrontation, rejection and suffering were inevitable. Yet his sufferings led to his resurrection and glorification. Jesus has "passed through the heavens," as the Letter to the Hebrews tells us, to take his rightful place at God's right hand. But he has not left us, rather through his Spirit, through prayer and the sacraments and through his love in us he has transformed us and made us sharers in his new life. He has made us into a new creation. "He has become the source of eternal life for all who obey him," the Letter to the Hebrews tells us. Or as Isaiah tells us: "By his stripes we were healed." Amen.

# Easter
## April 4, 2010

HOMILY – (Acts 10:34a, 36-43; Colossians 3:1-4; John 20:1-18) A pastor was telling some of the little children in school about Jesus' arrest and crucifixion. As he was teaching them about some of Jesus' last words on the cross, he asked: "What was the last thing Jesus said before he died?" One little child raised his hand and answered, "Jesus said: 'I'll be back'."

It's not recorded that Jesus said that on the cross, but there were several times that Jesus did predict his resurrection. Evidently the Jewish religious leaders remembered Jesus' prediction. So that his apostles could not steal his body and then try to tell people he was raised from the dead, Matthew tells us that after Jesus was buried, the chief priests and Pharisees asked Pilate to provide a guard at Jesus' tomb. The Apostles, however, thought the idea of resurrection was ridiculous and they were dumbfounded by the reports of the women and by the fact that Jesus' body was gone from the tomb.

Except perhaps the Roman guard, no one saw Jesus rise. The guards were bribed into telling the story that they fell asleep, and while they were asleep the apostles stole Jesus' body. Many times artists, who have tried to picture the resurrection, show the soldiers sleeping, which is unfortunate because it inaccurately portrays what the resurrection might have been like. The story that the soldiers were asleep is a contradiction in itself, because if they were asleep how could they say what had happened. This is not to mention the fact that if a Roman soldier fell asleep on his watch he could have lost his life for dereliction of duty.

Since the empty tomb is so much a part of the gospel

account of the resurrection, I would like to say a little more about the tomb. When I was in Israel, I had the good fortune of visiting Jesus' tomb at a time when there weren't many tourists around. I got to spend a considerable amount of time praying there. There is strong evidence, based on the tradition of the Jerusalem Christian community, that the place we honor today in the Church of the Holy Sepulcher as the tomb of Jesus is authentic. It was a place where the earliest Christians celebrated liturgies until the Romans destroyed Jerusalem. Then in 135 A.D. the emperor Hadrian filled in the area with tons of earth so he could build a temple to the goddess Aphrodite on that spot. Aphrodite's shrine remained there for 200 years until Constantine was converted and wanted to build a church to honor the place where Jesus was buried. The Christian community told him exactly where he would find Jesus' tomb. They pointed to the pagan temple and said Jesus' tomb is buried deep under that temple. In order to build his church, Constantine faced a double expense – he had to tear down the temple and then excavate the area. The Church historian and eyewitness Eusebius tells us in his Life of Constantine: "At once the work was carried out, and, as layer after layer of the subsoil came into view, the venerable and most holy memorial of the Savior's resurrection, beyond all our hopes, came into view." (from *The Holy Land* by Jerome Murphy-O'Connor, pg 45).

An empty tomb, even with such a positive argument about its authenticity, does not give absolute evidence of the resurrection for the resurrection can be known only by faith. Our faith is based on the witness of those who saw Christ after the resurrection. These witnesses had nothing to gain materially from the witness they gave and many of them, as we know, backed up their witness by the sacrifice of lives. We must mention too that our faith is also based on the gift of the Holy Spirit that Jesus gives us. For it is only through the Spirit that we can come to believe.

We have a saying, "seeing is believing." Thomas the Apostle took that approach as we will hear next week. But for most of us, it's the other way around. As we believe in the risen Christ, we begin to see him active in our lives, helping us, comforting us, guiding us. As we believe in the risen Christ, we begin to see him in others. My faith in the resurrection of Christ gave me the great comfort of knowing I am never fully alone but that Christ is always with me. My faith in the risen Christ made me more willing to spend time with him in prayer.

The resurrection is not just a belief that we pull out at Easter or a comforting doctrine we console ourselves with at a time of death. It is a whole way of life, a life that begins with our baptism and is sustained by our gathering in faith with the risen Christ on this day of his resurrection, the first day of the week. It is a way of life in which we try to keep ourselves aware of his presence in us in all we say and do throughout the week.

Today we are reminded of a truth most basic to our faith. Today we rededicate ourselves to living that faith in union with our risen Lord so we may one day come to share fully in his risen life. Amen.

## Second Sunday of Easter
### April 11, 2010

**INTRODUCTION** – (Acts 5:12-16; Rev. 1:9-11a, 12-13, 17-19; John 20:19-31) I want to start with some comments about our second reading. It is from the first chapter of the book of Revelation. I was discussing this book recently with a group of friends and one of them said that for him Revelations is the book he most dislikes in the Bible. He said it writes about so many terrible things happening. It does indeed, but throughout the book is all about hope . It was written during a time of severe persecution. Its message is that in the end evil would not prevail but Christ would be victorious over every form of evil. We will hear brief sections of this book for the next several weeks, sections that emphasize hope and salvation. John the Apostle, the author of Revelations, tells us in today's passage how the book came to be written. John was in exile on a little island called Patmos as punishment for preaching about Jesus. The risen Jesus appeared to him and began to reveal to him that those suffering for their faith in Jesus would share in Jesus' victory over evil and death. Unfortunately, part of the powerful vision describing Jesus was left out of our reading today.

Our first reading from the Acts of the Apostles describes for us how the risen Christ continues his saving work through the Apostles and through the community of those who believed in him.

**HOMILY** – A mother took her little three year old son to Mass for the first time. The child got impatient waiting for Mass to start. Turning to his mother the boy asked, "When does Jesus get here?"

I wonder if this was what the Apostle Thomas was asking himself all week. The other Apostles had seen the Lord on Easter Sunday evening. Thomas, for one reason or another, missed out on this first appearance of Jesus to the Apostles. Jesus did not appear again until the following Sunday. It's not surprising that it was not until the following Sunday that Jesus appeared. In a very short time, Sunday became the day when those who believed in Christ would come together in prayer and in celebration of the Eucharist. I will say more about Thomas later.

I just want to point out a couple of other features about today's gospel that I think are particularly noteworthy. For me personally, the way Jesus greeted his Apostles proved to be extremely important: "Peace be with you." In my early years as a priest I experienced a lot of depression and I prayed for peace. Being aware that Christ wanted us to have peace in our hearts, I was able to pray for peace with absolute confidence that I would eventually experience it. The assurance that Christ wanted peace for us kept me from giving up on my prayer until I received a positive answer to it.

The gospel goes on to show us Jesus sending his Apostles out in the power of the Spirit to bring Christ's peace to the world through the forgiveness of sins. Jesus said to them again: "Peace be with you. As the Father has sent me so I send you." Then he breathed his Spirit on them and said, "Receive the Holy Spirit. Whose sins you forgive are forgiven them?" Pope John Paul was so inspired by this passage that he designated this Sunday as "Divine Mercy Sunday." It's not that this is the only time God offers his mercy to us, but it is a good time to reflect that God's mercy is always available to us whenever we turn to him for forgiveness. The sacrament of reconciliation, which Christ gave to the Church, is a great help to us to receive his peace and his mercy.

Also in today's gospel we hear the story of Thomas who was not there on Easter Sunday night. I always wonder what made him stay around and wait for what seemed an impossibility to him – that Jesus was truly risen. When the other Apostles told him they had seen the Lord why didn't he just walk out and say, "They're all out of their minds." Something made him stay – maybe the little faith he had left held him there; maybe he had to prove to himself that he was right and everyone else was crazy.

It was good that Thomas didn't walk away, for when Jesus appeared on the Sunday after Easter, he made an act of faith in Jesus that was more profound than anything that had been said of Jesus by any of the Apostles up to that time. It wasn't just an act of faith that Jesus had risen, for he could see that, but he professed Jesus was "My Lord and my God." We have the advantage of thinking of God in terms of the Trinity, as Father, Son and Holy Spirit. We may not understand the mystery but we have the terminology. The Apostles did not think in this theological terminology – at least not right away; it took time for them to accept that somehow the Father was God and at the same time Jesus was God, but Jesus was not the Father and yet there was only one God. So, knowing their limited knowledge, Thomas' act of faith was awesome; Thomas knew somehow that Jesus was God, the God the Jewish people had worshipped for almost 2000 years. If Thomas had been asked how this could be, he would have been lost for an explanation, but he knew it was so. That was indeed great faith.

Jesus affirmed Thomas and spoke a blessing for all of us who have come to believe in him. "Blessed are those who have not seen and have believed." I see this blessing especially applicable to the Eucharist. We do not see Christ, but we believe his word: "This is my body." "This is my blood." I truly believe this is one of the biggest challenges to people's faith today. "Blessed are those who have not seen and have believed." Amen.

# Third Sunday of Easter
## April 18, 2010

INTRODUCTION – (Acts 5:27-32, 40b-41; Rev. 5:11-14; John 21:1-19) The risen Lord continues to be the focus of all of our Scripture readings today. In the second reading, John, the author of the Book of Revelation, has been trying to describe an ecstatic vision he had of heaven. John described God seated on his heavenly throne with 24 elders and four living creatures and countless angels surrounding God's throne. God had in his hand a scroll. The scroll is a central focus of the book for it reveals what is to come. The scroll was sealed shut with seven seals and no one of all those assembled before God's throne could open the scroll, no one except the risen Christ who is described as a lamb that had been killed — killed but who was victorious over every form of evil: even sin and death. Our second reading today (a short one) is a song from every creature in heaven and earth praising God the Father and the victorious Lamb of God, the risen Lord, who could open up the scroll. It is worth pointing out that the Lamb on the front of our altar is the symbol of the victorious and risen Christ from the Book of Revelation.

Today's first reading is taken from the Acts of the Apostles. After the ascension, Jesus continued his healing ministry through the apostles. On one occasion, Peter and John healed a man who was lame and they attributed the healing to the power of the risen Lord Jesus. This led to their arrest for preaching about Jesus and they were given a warning not to speak about Jesus again. A second time they were arrested and were thrown in jail, but an angel set them free. They went right on preaching about Jesus. So they were arrested for the third time and this is where things are when we hear today's first reading. The apostles Peter and John are on trial before the Sanhedrin, which was for the Jews their supreme religious authority made up of 71 members of the Sadducees, the Pharisees and the high priestly families. It seems strange to me that today's passage leaves out a few verses at the end of the reading that tell us that as a punishment for disobeying the authorities, the apostles were scourged before they were set free. What is remarkable is they were joyful in that they suffered for the Lord.

**HOMILY** – One perfectly beautiful Sunday morning, a priest couldn't resist the urge to go fishing. So he called up the bishop and with a fake raspy voice he told the bishop he was too sick to say the morning Masses, would the bishop send a substitute to say the Masses? Which the bishop did. The priest's first catch was the biggest fish he had ever landed. St. Peter, up in heaven, saw this and said to Jesus, "that priest lied and let down his congregation. How can you reward him like that?" Jesus smiled and said "actually I intend to teach him a lesson. After running out on his responsibilities as he did, is there anyone he can brag to about his big fish?"

I think today's gospel ranks way up there as one of the most affectionate and caring gospels that we know. I can just picture the apostles being out all night working feverishly tossing in their nets and pulling them back into the boat over and over all night and coming in to shore with nothing to show for all their labor. And there is Jesus, watching them come in, almost as if he had been there all night watching over them. He sees their exhaustion and frustration. He greets them as little children (which in this case is a term of affection toward one who is treasured in the way a parent treasures a child). He asks them the normal question people tend to ask fishermen: "Did you have any luck?" Then he filled their net with fish. When they finally got to shore, he had breakfast going for them. This was not just a thoughtful gesture; it expressed the real reason why he came to us – in order to feed us. Today's miracle recalls an earlier miracle, the miracle of the loaves and the fishes which took place beside this same lake, a miracle with a definite connection to the Eucharist. On that earlier occasion when Jesus fed the people miraculously, he made clear to them that he did not come just to deliver free meals for people but to be our food for everlasting life. "I am the living bread that came down from heaven; whoever eats this bread will live forever," he told us in John, 6:51.

Then our gospel moves on to Jesus' conversation with Peter, a conversation that lovingly gives Peter the opportunity to undo the three times he denied Jesus after Jesus' arrest. First Jesus asked Peter, "do you love me more than these?" You might recall that at the Last Supper, after Jesus predicted that everyone would desert him, Peter boasted "Though all may have their faith in you shaken, mine will never be." (Mt 26:33) Peter is more humble now as he answers Jesus: "you know that I love you." It is interesting the words Jesus and Peter use for love. In the Greek (the original version of the gospel) Jesus asks the first two times with agápe love (the highest form of love, love that expresses total unselfish devotion); Peter answers with philía love (a friendship, affectionate kind of love but not with the unselfish dedication of agápe love).

Finally the third time Jesus asks Peter if he loves him as a friend (philía), as if to say, "I'll accept whatever love you have to offer, Peter." You might recall that earlier in John's gospel Jesus identified himself as the Good Shepherd. Notice in today's gospel, Jesus transferred to Peter Jesus' own office as the Good Shepherd. After each time Jesus questioned Peter and Peter answered, Jesus said, "feed my lambs, feed my sheep." Peter's service to Christ's flock must be a loving gift of oneself as all service to God's people should be. Although Peter was distressed that Jesus questioned him for the third time, I am sure Peter felt totally assured of Jesus' forgiveness after this interchange. Peter did serve Jesus and Jesus' flock with agape – totally unselfish love – for he gave his life for Christ and his Church.

May we now continue to praise Christ's victory over sin and death and may we love Christ and one another with a love that expresses unselfish devotion. Amen.

# Fourth Sunday of Easter
## April 25, 2010

**INTRODUCTION** – (Acts 13:14, 43-52; Rev. 7:9, 14b-17; John 10:27-30) The Book of Revelation requires a lot of explanation, which we do not have time for – but at least I want to give some background so today's second reading won't be a total mystery. Last week we heard John, the author of Revelation, describe some of what he saw in his vision of heaven. God had in his hand a scroll on which was written what was to take place in the future, but the scroll was sealed with seven seals. Only the Lamb of God, that is the Risen Jesus, was able to open the seals. That was last week's reading. John went on to tell us that as the seals were opened, war and terror revealed themselves. The Book of Revelation does not relish this kind of horror; it was only telling what was to happen, and indeed it keeps on happening. The intent of Revelation is to offer hope to those who suffer, especially those who suffer for being faithful to Christ. This is where today's reading takes us. One of the 24 elders standing before God's throne interprets more of John's vision of heaven. John sees God's holy people surrounding God's throne and praising him. They are dressed in white symbolizing their inner holiness and they are holding palm branches as a symbol of their sharing in Christ's victory over sin and death. Their sufferings are over, God will protect them, and the Lamb of God will shepherd them and provide for all their needs.

Our first reading takes us to Antioch in Pisidia, a small city in what is today the central part of Turkey. Paul is on his first missionary journey accompanied by his companion Barnabas. Jewish communities were scattered all throughout the Roman Empire. Paul made two visits to the local Jewish synagogue there. His first visit was so successful that when he returned the following week he filled the house. But his second visit wasn't nearly so successful as we will now hear.

**HOMILY** – Archbishop Dolan, the current Archbishop of New York, tells this story. When he was a seminarian in Rome, one day he saw Bishop Sheen coming from an audience with Pope Paul VI. A crowd gathered around Bishop Sheen and asked him what the Holy Father said to him. Bishop Sheen blushed a little and said: "The Holy Father told me: 'Fulton Sheen, you will have a high place in heaven.'" Someone else asked how Bishop Sheen replied to the pope. The witty Bishop Sheen said: "Your Holiness, would you mind making that into an infallible statement?" (from *Preaching Resources*, April 25, 2010, published by Celebration Publications, Kansas City, Mo.)

I guess we all would like insurance that we're going to get into heaven, but if we did, I wonder if we would keep trying very hard to get there. At least we have the assurance that if we faithfully follow our Good Shepherd, we don't have to worry about it. Jesus tells us in today's gospel: "My sheep hear my voice; I know them, and they follow me. I give them eternal life, and they shall never perish. No one can take them out of my hand."

Good Shepherd Sunday always reminds me of a person I counseled many years ago. She was very anxious and depressed and this image of the Good Shepherd was her favorite image of Jesus. It always helped her to feel safe and secure when she thought of the Good Shepherd. Each one of us is important to him. The Good Shepherd said he would lay down his life for his sheep, and he has; he has also overcome death and through grace we share in his victory. That is the image given to us in the second reading of a great crowd, beyond anyone's ability to count, being led by the Lamb to springs of life-giving water. The last line in that reading is very touching: "God (like a loving parent) will wipe every tear from their eyes."

I would like to make a brief reference to the sacrament of Confirmation. Today Archbishop Pilarczyk will be here to confirm eight of our children. The past two times we had confirmation the Archbishop allowed me to do them, because I am the dean of the Cathedral Deanery. This time, however, he said, "You should have a bishop come there sometimes." He probably wants to see if we're taking good care of St. Boniface. Confirmation is probably the least understood of the seven sacraments and that's why I wanted to say a few words about it. We learned from our catechism that Baptism and Confirmation mark us with an invisible but indelible seal as belonging to God. The significant difference between Baptism and Confirmation is that in Baptism we become God's child, we are reborn, we receive God's grace for the first time but we are spiritually like infants. When we are Confirmed, we are strengthened in that grace and we are called to live our life in Christ in a more mature way. The analogy I am making is between birth and adulthood. When we are babies we are on the receiving end of life, we need to be cared for and nurtured. When we are adults we reach out of ourselves, we give life to others both biologically through having children and emotionally through our care and concern for others. So Confirmation calls us to reach out of ourselves, to bring God's life to others through our prayers for them and through sharing our faith and our love with them. The Holy Spirit is given to us in a special way enabling us to do that. Of course, a great deal more could be said about Confirmation and about the Holy Spirit that is given to us, but what I have said might just be enough to remind all of us what we have been called to be when we received Confirmation. Perhaps this might move us in our prayers to pray for those who are being confirmed today. We pray they, and we, follow our Good Shepherd faithfully. Through the way we live our lives, may we witness to our love for God and thus help others to know him and to love him. Amen.

## Fifth Sunday of Easter
### May 2, 2010

**INTRODUCTION** – (Acts 14:21-27; Rev. 21:1-5a; John 13:31-33a, 34-45) Last Sunday we heard a little bit about Paul's first missionary journey. He led many Jews and Pagans to faith in Jesus as the Messiah, while at the same time arousing much opposition. In today's first reading we are still with Paul as he makes his return trip back to the Christian Community in Syria which had originally inspired and sponsored his mission. In spite of the harsh treatment he had previously received from his opponents in those places, he is not afraid to revisit cities where he had already preached. The name Antioch could confuse us for there were two cities named Antioch. The first mention of Antioch was a town in central Turkey where a mob of unbelievers ran Paul out of town. The second Antioch (the place where his missionary journey began) was on the east coast of Syria and it was one of the four largest cities in the Roman Empire. Paul was returning there to report on the successes and challenges of his mission. He acknowledged that at times it wasn't easy: "It is necessary for us to undergo many hardships to enter the kingdom of God."

HOMILY – After giving her catechism class a very thorough lesson on the Ten Commandments, the teacher quizzed her students. "What is the First Commandment?" she asked. She called on a boy who was staring into space. She knew he hadn't been paying attention to the lesson. The boy thought a bit and answered: "The First Commandment was when Eve told Adam to eat the apple." (from *Preaching Resources*, May 2, 2010, published by Celebration Publications, Kansas City, Mo.)

This one comes from *Reader's Digest*, May, 2010, pg 176. A lady asked her friend if she attended Church. Her friend just shook her head. "I haven't gone in a long time. I'm sure I'm a lost soul anyway. I've probably already broken all seven commandments."

I'll say more about commandments in a moment, but there is something I want to say first. Has it ever happened that you, as it has to me, to tell a joke and forget the punch line or try to tell a story and couldn't remember the ending? Without the punch line or a good ending to a story the hearers are left wondering, "What's that all about?" We are coming to the end of the book of Revelation where we find the main point of this Book. Sure, the Book of Revelation predicts war and suffering and turmoil – often in symbolic ways that are very frightening. The study of history confirms the dire predictions of this Book. Turmoil and suffering are part of life in this world. When Paul says in the second reading that we have to undergo many hardships in order to enter God's kingdom, is he's saying that we will never face hardship if we choose not to follow Jesus? Of course not. It's just that following Jesus has its own unique set of difficulties. I believe that those who do not have Jesus in their lives suffer even greater difficulties because they do not share his wisdom and experience his love. Turmoil and suffering, which touch every person's life are not the main point of the Book of Revelation. The main point of Revelation is victory, victory for those who have faithfully followed Christ. Our second reading today begins this last part of Revelation. It describes, as best it can and in a symbolic way, the new heavens and new earth that God is creating.

One avenue that leads to that new work of God's creation is the new commandment he gives us, "As I have loved you, so you also should love one another." You might wonder what's new about this? Here's what's new: we who are human are commanded to love in a divine way; we are to love like the Son of God has loved us. How can we do something that is so far above our nature? It would be like teaching a worm to recite Shakespeare. It seems impossible. Jesus would not ask the impossible of us. We can love with a divine love only when we have God in our hearts helping us to love in that way. The consequence of that kind of love in us will be that we will share in God's peace and God's joy, a peace like the world cannot give and a joy that is God's own. "I have told you this so that my joy might be in you and your joy might be complete." (John 15:11) For all this to happen, it follows that we need to stay connected with Christ and allow him to live in us. He does so in a powerful and unique way through the Eucharist we now celebrate. Amen.

# Sixth Sunday of Easter
## May 9, 2010

**INTRODUCTION** – (Acts 15:1-2, 22-29; Revelation 21:10-14, 22-23; John 14:23-29) The Apostles and all who first came to believe in Jesus were Jewish. They did not see themselves as part of a new religion; thus they continued to follow their Jewish laws, customs, rituals and traditions. However, there were problems when Gentiles started to believe in Jesus. Many Jews who believed in Jesus insisted that Gentiles had to adopt Jewish ways if they wanted to consider themselves followers of Jesus. So when our first reading speaks of circumcision, its really talking about all the rules and customs the Jews were bound to follow. This conflict arose especially in Antioch, in Syria, because it was a large city and racially quite diverse. To solve the problem, the leaders of the Church at Antioch, including St. Paul, went to Jerusalem to meet with some of the other Apostles. Their decision was sent back to Antioch. It was a major decision affecting how the Church would grow, including whether we would have faith in Christ today and how we would be living it. Notice how the Apostles introduced their decision: "It is the decision of the Holy Spirit, and ours too" This has always been the belief of the Church whenever the bishops gather in council together with the Holy Father that the Church is being guided by the Holy Spirit. It is an important concept especially today when so many people think they can make up their own rules and do not need the Church to tell them what's right or wrong.

**HOMILY** – Happy Mothers' Day. I'll start with a little joke, then a reflection on mothers, before my thoughts on today's readings. A little girl, when asked her name, would always tell people "I'm Mr. Brown's daughter." One day her mother told her, "Don't say to people you're 'Mr. Brown's daughter.' Tell them 'I'm Susan Brown.'" One Sunday morning, as the new pastor was getting acquainted with his parishioners, he asked the little girl: "Aren't you Mr. Brown's daughter?" The little girl answered, "I thought I was, but my mom tells me I'm not." (From *The Joyful Noiseletter*, May, 2004) When children quote us, sometimes it can be embarrassing – one of the joys and challenges of raising children.

Reflection: "God gave the world stars and there was beauty. God gave the world sun and there was warmth. God gave the world rain and there was life. God gave the world mothers and there was love." (From *The Joyful Noiseletter*, May, 2008)

One more little piece of information: I read recently that a middle-income family can expect to spend $291,570 to raise a child born in 2008 to adulthood. The estimate covers food, shelter, and other necessities for an infant until age 18, but does not include the cost of childbirth or college. (From *Leadership Network Advance* 9/22/09) Parents make quite an investment in choosing to be a parent, and especially it is a mind-boggling investment if one parent has to go it alone – usually the mother. We thank our mothers today (and those who have the role of mothers) for their dedication and the many, many sacrifices they make in their vocation.

I've been talking about the Book of Revelation for the last several weeks. Since we have reached the climax of the Book, it would be negligent of me not to say anything about it today. John, the author of the Book, has a vision of heaven, the source of hope for a people who were suffering for their belief in Christ. Today's reading gives us just a hint of what heaven will be like – expressed symbolically as the new and eternal Jerusalem. The author has to use symbols because it will be so much a "new heaven and a new earth" that there's no way we could ever grasp what it might be like while we are still part of this world.

Today's reading tells us the new Jerusalem has a massive, high wall around it. At one time all large cities were encircled by walls for security from wild animals and hostile neighbors. In another part of Revelations, we are told these walls were 1500 miles high, and each of the four walls were 1500 miles in length thus forming a perfect cube. The wall was over 200 feet thick. Does that speak security to you? The foundation stones for the wall were various gems on which the names of the twelve apostles were written, showing the city is founded on the apostles. Notice there are twelve gates. The gates of the city, open in all four directions, indicate that God's kingdom is open to all people. The gates are each made of a single pearl (thus the term, "pearly gates"). The gates have inscribed on them the names of the twelve tribes of Israel indicating the Old Testament roots of our faith. The dimensions of the city would be about half the size of the United States! That's some city. The size, which for the people of those days must have seemed infinite, symbolizes the multitude of people that will fill God's kingdom. The city was beautiful beyond belief. The city is without a temple which says we will experience God directly. No temple will be needed. It needs no light for its source of light is God and Jesus, God's victorious Son, who is the fullness of light. Much more is said about heaven in the last two chapters of the book. It is where we all hope to be some day.

Today's gospel gives us a map, as it were, to direct us to this new creation God is preparing for those who love him. Jesus tells us, "whoever loves me will keep my word, and my Father will love him and we will come to him and make our dwelling with him." What this means is if we want to some day dwell in the new and eternal Jerusalem, it has to begin in this world with God's dwelling in us. That union between God and ourselves will constitute the true joy of heaven. Jesus tells us today, having God dwell in us involves keeping Jesus' word. Jesus goes on to explain the special help we will have to enable us to keep his word. "The Advocate, the Holy Spirit, whom the Father will send in my name, will teach you everything and remind you of all that I told you." The word "teach" really jumped out at me. To their credit, I've met so many people who want to be close to God and they want to experience God, but they want it almost instantaneously. Just by saying a prayer or receiving a sacrament, they want God to somehow magically transform them. They're looking for a short cut to help them avoid all the effort of learning and growing into what God wants of us. They want it all right now – heaven and all the wonderful feeling of knowing God intimately. But this word "teach" tells us something else. Growing in knowing and loving God, growing in loving others in a more unselfish way, growing in the ability to pray, growing in holiness takes patience and time and effort. It's an effort that brings many rewards, but it's not automatic and not without challenges. The Holy Spirit will teach us if we want to learn, if we don't give up too soon. God dwelling in us and our dwelling with him is the true joy that awaits us.

# Feast of the Ascension
## May 16, 2010

**INTRODUCTION** – (Acts 1:1-11; Ephesians 1:17-23; Luke 24:40-53) St. Luke gave us two books in the New Testament: The Acts of the Apostles and, of course, his gospel. We hear from both of them today. The gospel ends with the ascension and the Acts of the Apostles begins with the ascension. You'll notice when you hear the first reading from the Acts, he refers to his gospel as his "first book." It is interesting how he treats the ascension in each of these two books. In the Acts he said Jesus ascended 40 days after Easter, but in his gospel he describes how Jesus appeared to his apostles Easter Sunday night, spoke with them, ate with them and then, that very night, he led them out to Bethany where he ascended into heaven. It seems as if Jesus' physical departure from the apostles and his return to the Father was not a one-time dramatic event. It was more like a process. One way of thinking of the 40-day period is that after the resurrection Jesus appeared rather frequently to the apostles. Luke's description of the ascension 40 days after Easter seems to mark the end of those frequent appearances. After that Jesus would be present to his followers invisibly through the Holy Spirit, the sacraments, and the Church. St. Luke described this invisible presence throughout the Acts of the Apostles.

**HOMILY** – A woman, who never came to Church except on Easter, came up to the pastor to complain: "I can't believe it! Every time I come here all they sing is 'Jesus Christ is Risen Today.'" (From *The Joyful Noiseletter*, April, 2001) We're not singing it today but it would be just as appropriate as if it were Easter because the ascension of Jesus is a major part of the mystery of his resurrection.

We say in our profession of faith each week that Jesus "ascended into heaven and is seated at the right hand of the Father." This image is an extremely important image in the Scriptures. Maybe it doesn't hit us as powerfully as it did the early Christians because we just take it for granted that that's where Jesus would be, at God's right hand. St. John tells us at the beginning of his gospel: "in the beginning was the Word and the Word was with God and the Word was God." Seated at the right hand of God is where he was before he came to earth as a human being and now he is once again enthroned in his proper place. For those who do not have the faith that we have, faith in the Trinity and in the Incarnation, the idea of Jesus seated at God's right hand would have been blasphemous. That was exactly the response of the high priest when Jesus was on trial and Jesus said to the high priest, "From now on you will see the Son of Man seated at the right hand of the Power" (a name they used for God since out of reverence the Jews did not speak God's name). (Mt. 26:64) The high priest cried out, "He has blasphemed." Let's think of what Jesus was saying for a moment. What if I said, "when you get to heaven you will see all the angels and saints and then you are going to see me seated with God at his right hand." You would rightly think that I was seriously deluded or greatly arrogant. This image expressed for Jesus' followers his everlasting greatness, and kingship and power and yes, his divinity. An amazing thought: a human being, just like us except without sin, is seated in the highest heaven, sharing in God's power and glory. When one of the first deacons, St. Stephen, was martyred he died with these words on his lips, "Behold, I see the heavens opened and the Son of Man standing at the right hand of God." (Acts 7:56) Paul expresses this belief with great emphasis in today's second reading – that God raised

Jesus from the dead and seated him at his right hand in the heavens, far above every power, every creature that has existed or could exist. All things are beneath his feet and he is head over everything. (Eph. 1:17-23)

Peter, in his first sermon after Pentecost, proclaimed a Jesus who was exalted at the right hand of God. (Acts 2:33) Paul repeats the image a number of times in his letters and so does the Letter to the Hebrews. We picture the ascension pretty much the way it is described in the Acts of the Apostles with Jesus disappearing behind a cloud, no more to be seen by mortal human beings, except by an occasional saint. Even though he is now hidden from our sight, the Scriptures want us to see him sharing God's power and glory. To know that our God, who has raised the human body of Jesus from the dead and taken him to sit at his right hand, has given him to the Church, to us, to be our salvation and to lead us to glory.

St. Luke gives us two ways of looking at the ascension. In our first reading the Apostles are looking longingly into the sky as Jesus disappears behind the clouds. In the gospel the Apostles return to Jerusalem with joy, knowing that their crucified Jesus now lived. In both accounts of the ascension they are told they would receive the Holy Spirit from Jesus, giving them the power to witness to the world the miracle of the resurrection. We can look at the ascension with longing or with joy, but either way we are left with a job to do, to witness to our faith in the risen and glorified Lord in whatever way we can.

# Seventh Sunday of Easter
## May 24, 1998

**INTRODUCTION** – (Acts 7:55-60; Rev 22:12-14, 16-17, 20; John 17:20-26) Thursday was the feast of the Ascension of Jesus into heaven. Our readings today flow from that idea. St. Stephen, the first martyr, is strengthened in his time of trial by a vision of Jesus in glory at the right hand of God the Father. The psalm refrain praises Christ who is king, the most high over all the earth. The second reading from the book of Revelation foretells the triumph of Christ our Lord over all evil and assures us that he will return again, soon.

The gospel is the last part of a magnificent prayer Jesus prayed at the Last Supper. After he prayed for his disciples, he prays for all of us who would come to believe in him through their preaching his gospel.

**HOMILY** – Today's gospel was part of Jesus' prayer at the Last Supper. Consider the fact that he is about to die. His final prayer we would expect would express those thoughts that are deepest in his own heart. The third part of his prayer is for all of us, all who will come to believe in him and follow him. And what does he pray for us? His prayer is for unity in love. And he prays for it over and over again. He prays that as he is one with the Father, we might be one with him and one with each other.

Our culture idealizes rugged individualism, the self-made man, the guy who pulls himself up by his own boot straps, the cowboy who rides off into the sunset alone, the person who doesn't need to depend on anyone. But the reality of our lives in today's world is that we need other people in hundreds of ways. We need others for everyday necessities, for education, for employment, for inspiration, for health needs and of course we need friends and family to support us emotionally.

In our spiritual life we need to know Christ in a personal way and to have him as a friend, we need to take time for private and individual prayer, but our relationship with our Lord can't just be an individual thing only. It can't just be something between me and God to the exclusion of anyone else. If we want to be one with Christ, we're going to be one with a lot of people too. Thomas Merton said it so clearly "Without love and compassion for others, our own apparent love for Christ is fiction." Christianity is essentially a community religion. If in so many areas of our everyday lives we need others, why do we think that in our spiritual lives we can get along just fine without anyone's help? Christ has made it clear that how we reach him and how he comes to us is through others: through Scripture, through liturgy, though the faith that is passed on by being taught and lived by a community of believers, through the sacraments and through how we treat one another, especially the least of his brothers and sisters. If we say we don't need the church, we don't need other people to help us get to God, we are trying to walk to the other side of the world with only one leg. I honestly think this is the biggest sin, the biggest heresy of the modern day, because those who disassociate themselves from the Church are disconnecting themselves from the roots that provide nourishment for their faith. Without deep roots and the spiritual nourishment we need, we become an easy pushover for the devil when a moment of weakness comes.

The unity that our Lord talks about presupposes some leadership. Someone has to be in charge. If you asked a dozen people to interpret some part of scripture, or to tell you what God thinks about some issue, you would probably get a dozen different answers. Someone has to have the last word if there is going to be some unity, or people will be going in a dozen different directions. Christ was no dummy. He knew that. He had a dozen Apostles with him all the time and he knew some of the debates and discussions they got into. He gave Peter the job to be the rock, the source of stability, the focus of unity, the one to hold them all together. Again we get back to the need for the Church and the way Christ established it if we are going to be faithful to Christ, and not just be going off on our own.

Our unity with each other is not just for our own personal well-being, but it affects in a most important way the whole saving work of our Lord. Our common belief, our common set of values, our oneness in prayer and most of all in love tell the world about Jesus. Jesus said, "I pray that they may be one in us, that the world may believe that you (Father) sent me." The church's mission, which means your mission as well as mine, is not just to save ourselves, but to bring God's saving grace and life to others too. Staying united is one of the primary ways we will do it. When we all go our own individual ways, our efforts become significantly less effective.

We're all together in this world; we're all together in our spiritual journey too. Jesus wants us to live as one with him and as one with each other. This was his greatest desire for us his followers. This is one of the experiences that mystics have described. Mystics, those who are closest to God, have an innate sense of how interconnected we all are. I want to tell you the story of an old man whose experience at the Washington Vietnam Veterans Memorial was somehow a mystical experience. He was weeping noticeably as he stood at the Memorial. Moved by the sight, a young man waked over to the old man, put his hand on his shoulder and said, "Is one of these yours, sir?" The old man said softly, "Not *one* of them, son! *All* of them!"

# Vigil of Pentecost
## May 22, 2010

**INTRODUCTION** – (Ezekiel 37:1-14; Romans 8:22-27; John 7:37-39) I hope you have the impression that today is a very special feast. We have a special Vigil Mass with its own readings and prayers. Christmas, Easter, the birth of John the Baptist, and the feast of the Assumption are the only other feasts that have a special Vigil Mass. There is a wider assortment of readings we can choose from than there is on an ordinary Sunday. I asked parishioners to wear the color red in honor of the Holy Spirit. If you were to go to Mass tomorrow, you would also see there is a sequence. The only other feast that has a sequence that is a required part of the liturgy is Easter. Today is the third most important feast in the Church year, the feast that celebrates the completion of Jesus' saving work with his sending of the Holy Spirit.

Our first reading today is one of my favorites. At the time of Ezekiel (600 BC), God's people did not have any idea of individual or personal resurrection. Ezekiel, in his vision of a field of dry bones, is referring to the nation of Israel that was at that time in Exile in Babylon. They had given up hope of ever returning home or of ever being a nation again. They thought their race and nation were dead. Ezekiel is telling them God would bring them back from exile and raise them up. I should also add, no one knew about the Trinity at that time in history. When Ezekiel refers to God's Spirit in today's first reading, he is referring to God's power to bring about life.

**HOMILY** – Today's gospel describes the Spirit as a river of living water. When John tells us, "there was no Spirit yet, because Jesus had not yet been glorified," he is not saying the Holy Spirit did not exist. He is saying the Holy Spirit had not yet been imparted to Jesus' followers.

They had to wait until Jesus ascended to the Father and sent the Holy Spirit upon them.

St. Cyril of Jerusalem, who lived in the fourth century, asked this question in his commentary on today's gospel: "Why did Christ call the grace of the Spirit water?" He answers the question this way: "Because all things are dependent on water; plants and animals have their origin in water." In other words: water brings life. It's that simple. Without water life cannot exist. When we recite the Creed, we profess that the Holy Spirit is the Lord and giver of life.

The Holy Spirit is our connection with Christ. It is through the Spirit that we share in Christ's life. This is one of the basic gifts the Spirit gives us, a sharing in Christ's life. As with any life, our life in Christ is meant to be an active life. When a person is alive but they are inactive, it is either that they spend too much time in front of the TV or they are comatose. When the Spirit makes us alive in Christ, the Spirit also gives us gifts that help this life in Christ to flourish. According to St. Paul, such gifts are love, joy, peace, patience, kindness, goodness, faithfulness, humility and self-control. (*Galatians 5:22 & 23*) The Spirit also gives us gifts to help us live that life in service of others – many of which are named in the letters of St. Paul. Another way the Spirit helps us is mentioned in tomorrow's gospel. Jesus told us the Spirit will teach us and remind us of all that Jesus taught us.

The Spirit helps us individually, but the Spirit also helps us in and through the Church. Before Jesus died he established a community of believers and gave that community teachers and leaders. It was on this community, which is the Church, that Jesus sent the Holy Spirit. (This is why Pentecost is considered the birthday of the Church.) The Spirit touches our lives through this community, through its beliefs, its values, its sacraments, its teachings and through our love for one another as members of the same body of Christ of which we are a part as St. Paul will tell us tomorrow.

Sometimes people drop away from their religion. They claim to be spiritual people, but they have little use for organized religion. We should not be surprised that people who are an active part of a religious organization are not perfect. Christ did call sinners to follow him. Those who abandon organized religion and claim to be "spiritual" may have forgotten that if they are living by God's Holy Spirit, the Spirit would be calling them to be one with other believers so they can share in the many ways the Spirit works through the Church. It was a major part of Christ's prayer at the Last Supper that his followers be one as he and the Father are one, and surely the Spirit would be prompting Jesus' followers to follow Christ's wishes. Sometimes I wonder when someone tells me they are spiritual, but they snub organized religion, whether it is the <u>Holy</u> Spirit whose lead they are following or the spirit of our times that is relatively careless about our responsibilities toward God.

In today's second reading Paul tells us how the Spirit helps us as we pray. One of the special ways the Spirit helps us in prayer is in the Eucharist. And so we continue on, asking the Holy Spirit to help us offer ourselves and our love to our heavenly Father.

# Trinity Sunday
## June 7, 2009

**INTRODUCTION** – (Proverbs 8:22-31; Romans 5:1-5; John 16:12-15) There are a number of books in the Old Testament called wisdom books. The books discuss topics such as the meaning of life or the meaning of suffering as well as practical idea on how to raise children or how to handle your money. Our first reading comes from one of the books in the wisdom tradition: the book of Proverbs. We tend to think of wisdom as a skill or as knowledge that contributes toward living a long and good life. The Jews sometimes described wisdom as a woman who tirelessly tries to lead people away from foolishness and sin. In today's reading wisdom is described as a person who was with God before creation and who helped God create the world. It does not describe the Trinity for that would have been incomprehensible to them at that time in history (about 500 BC) but, with our knowledge of the Trinity, we can see a vague foreshadowing of what was to be revealed at a later time through Jesus.

**HOMILY** – Today we encounter the mystery of all mysteries, the mystery that underlies our faith and our entire spiritual lives. It is a mystery too great for many people to accept. Many people prefer having a God whom they can understand. My suspicion is that if God is someone I can completely understand, someone probably made him up. I think we should not be surprised that the God who made all things is greater than all things, including our human intellect.

I have been spending a lot of time in the past several months thinking about why we believe in a Trinity. The only answer for the source of our belief in the Trinity is in what Jesus did and said and as it is recorded for us in the New Testament. The NT never used the word Trinity. That word was coined by Tertullian, a Christian philosopher who was born about 115-120 years after Jesus died. Tertullian coined this word "Trinity" as he was trying to find a way to put into words the faith of the early Church about Christ. Jesus certainly showed himself to be a unique person. The question was "how unique?" He spoke with authority and originality. He spoke of God as "my Father," sometimes even using a term that a child might use to address his or her father, "Abba." Speaking only as God could speak, he forgave sins, he authoritatively interpreted the Law of Moses, he made demands on people such as forbidding divorce, loving and forgiving even one's enemies, he worked marvelous signs and he acted against evil with amazing power. "Thomas's profession of faith, 'My Lord and my God,' summed up the impact that Jesus as the risen Lord had on the majority of his followers." (*God, Engaging Theology: Catholic Perspectives* by Joseph A. Bracken, pg 6) After his resurrection, starting with Peter on Pentecost, his followers claimed that Jesus sat at the right hand of God and he poured the Spirit upon his disciples (something only God could do). A creed we say if we say the rosary, the Apostles' Creed, goes back almost to the time of the Apostles. How could one claim that Jesus was divine? This was a revolutionary idea that Jesus, a laborer from the backwater town of Nazareth who had been condemned and executed as a criminal, and whom his followers claimed to see alive three days later, was the same as the God who created the world, the same God whom the Jews had worshipped for almost 2000 years. If Jesus were God, and the one he called "Father" were God, how could that be? How could one express this belief. Many of his followers tried, including people whose names were Origin, Tertullian, Arius, St. Athenatius, St. Hilary of Potier, St. Cyril of Jerusalem, St. Basil the Great, St. Gregory of Nyssa, St. Gregory of Nazienzen, St. Augustine, just to name a few. It took almost three hundred years of discussion and controversy, with some ideas being accepted, others being rejected, not to mention there was some bloodshed over this issue.

(People took theology seriously in those days!) It wasn't until 325, in an effort to keep peace in his empire, Constantine called the bishops together to Nicaea to define this relationship between Jesus and God the Father. Fifty-six years later another council was called, the Council of Constantinople, to further clarify and expand on the Council of Nicaea. The Council of Constantinople defined the Holy Spirit, whom Jesus spoke about and Paul wrote about, as the third person of the Trinity. That is the Creed that we profess every Sunday.

St. Augustine gave us seven statements about the Trinity that doesn't take away the mystery but it describes it very simply: "The Father is God, the Son is God, the Holy Spirit is God; the Father is not the Son, the Son is not the Holy Spirit, the Holy Spirit is not the Father; there is only one God." The Father, Son and Spirit are three separate persons, but so closely bound together that they are one God. What is the bond that truly unites persons? It is love. So when John tells us God is love, he is telling us how this can be: three person in one divine being, equal in every way, but differing from one another in their relationship with each other.

It is into that loving union that we are invited through the gift of God's life that comes to us through grace. It is through our love for God and for one another, through prayer and through the sacraments that our union with God deepens. Some day it will all come together for us and make sense, but until it does we walk by faith. We are blessed to be able to express that faith in our Mass today as we offer to our heavenly Father the perfect sacrifice of Jesus, our brother, through the power of the Holy Spirit. Amen.

# Body & Blood of Christ
## June 6, 2010

**INTRODUCTION** – (Genesis 14:18-20; 1 Corinthians 11:23-26; Luke 9:11b-17) Today's first reading takes us to the Holy Land about 1850 years before Christ. Abraham's nephew, Lot, had been captured by some local tribes and Abraham set out to rescue him, which he did. On his return, he passed by Salem, which is Jerusalem today. He was met by Melchizedek, who was both king and high priest in that district. It was not unusual for the same person to be both king and high priest. Melchizedek offered bread and wine. It is hard to know whether it was offered as refreshment to Abraham or it was offered as a sacrifice to God Most High. At any event, some of the early fathers in the Church saw this gesture as a foreshadowing of the Eucharist. (Our stained-glass window on the side depicts this scene.)

The second reading from St. Paul is especially significant in that the Letter to the Corinthians was written 10 to 15 years before the earliest gospel; thus our second reading is the oldest description of the Eucharist that is known today. The language Paul uses indicates this is a tradition that is authentic and reliable. He received it from the Lord and he has handed it on to the Corinthians as he had received it. Receiving it "from the Lord" does not necessarily mean that he received it directly, but that it is an essential part of the gospel and has its origin in the teaching and the life of Jesus Christ.

**HOMILY** – In the early days of our country before the Civil War, ministers on the frontier used to do a lot of traveling to preach the gospel. One particular preacher would go from place to place doing revivals. He always traveled with an assistant who did the cooking, took care of the horses, set things up for the revival, etc. One day he was going to a pretty remote area and he said to his assistant, "You've heard me preach so many times I'll bet you could give the talk tonight. I could use a little break. No one knows what I look like way out here." (You see, TV hadn't been invented yet.) His assistant agreed, so they traded attire and the assistant dressed like the preacher and vice versa. The assistant did a fabulous job and at the end asked if there were any questions. One member of the congregation asked a very difficult question about predestination. The preacher's helper knew he was in a tight spot, thought for a minute and said, "Well, sir, that's such an easy question, I'll bet my assistant can answer that for you." Things are not always as they appear to be.

Last Sunday we celebrated the Feast of the Holy Trinity – a great mystery. Today we celebrate another great mystery: the real presence of Jesus under the form of bread and wine in the Eucharist. I honestly think this mystery is more difficult for many people to accept than the mystery of the Trinity. Yet it is clearly expressed in all four gospels and in St. Paul's letter to the Corinthians. Although the Last Supper account in John's gospel does not include the institution of the Eucharist, John's gospel gives us a much expanded teaching on the Eucharist early in his gospel right after he tells us about Jesus' miracle of feeding the multitude.

I think people have trouble believing in the Eucharist primarily because four of our five senses report that the bread we receive and the cup we drink are still bread and wine. Our sense of hearing, however, tells us the bread and wine are no longer ordinary bread and wine. They are different after they are blessed. Our ears hear the words of Jesus: "This is my body," "this is my blood . . .do this in memory of me."

If we can believe that the Son of God could come to

us as human, should it be any more difficult to believe that the Son of God could come to us as our food and drink. Things are not always as they appear to be. My story at the beginning was one example of this. Let me give you another: we might have a vitamin pill and an M&M that look exactly the same. We know, however, one has the power to help keep us healthy and the other just gives us a few calories that we probably don't need. What something looks like is not always an indication of the quality or quantity of power that is contained within it. There is power in our daily food to nourish for a short time, but the food Jesus offers has power to prepare us and nourish us for eternal glory. Jesus said in John's gospel, "Do not work for food that perishes but for the food that endures for eternal life, which the Son of Man will give you." (Jn 6:27)

We come to Mass to be fed, for we need to feed our spirits with spiritual food as we feed our bodies with regular food. In addition to Mass there are other opportunities to be nourished spiritually here at St. Boniface, but I want to highlight one in particular. Every week we have two holy hours. Deacon Jerry usually does the one on Wednesday mornings after Mass and I usually do the one on Friday afternoon. At a holy hour we expose the Blessed Sacrament on the altar in a monstrance (a decorated vessel which allows us to see the host). The purpose of this is to help us renew our faith in Christ's presence and to offer prayers and adoration to Jesus for his presence with us in this way. We always say the rosary, part of the Divine Office, a few other prayers and then have benediction. Although we call it a holy hour it usually lasts about 50 minutes. This time of prayer can be very nourishing spiritually. Sometimes we have only a half-dozen people here. I would love to see more people come. I wish to invite you to come. I'm sure we all pray for certain things. In conclusion, I pray that today's feast may revitalize and renew in us our faith in the Eucharist and our love for Christ's presence with us. Amen.

# 10th Sunday in Ordinary Time
## June 11, 1989

HOMILY – (1 Kings 17:17-24; Galatians 1:11-19; Luke 7:11-17) We are made helpless by the reality of death. We say at the time: "I'm sorry." or "Let me offer you my sympathy." About all we can do is offer support. Jesus on the other hand could walk into the most distressing situation and turn it completely around.

There is nothing that tears me up more than the death of a young person. In the gospel story the tragedy was compounded by the current social situation. A woman in that culture had no means of sustenance if she did not have a father or husband or son to provide for her. How helpless and sad any one of us would have felt if we had encountered this funeral procession leaving the city.

Yet Jesus has the nerve to go up to the woman and tell her "do not cry"! Then he touches the litter holding the young man who had died and he tells him to get up. When he does, he brings him back to his mother. Everyone is overwhelmed. A sense of fear fills them, not the kind of fear that makes a person want to run away, but this is more a sense of awe, knowing that one is in the presence of GOD! So there is no running away, only praising: "A great prophet has risen among us and God has visited his people."

There are so many ways to look at today's reading. We see the compassion of Jesus, his tenderness and caring, especially for those in the most desperate of situations. We see the power of his word, a word that gives life. We see the meaning of Jesus' work, why he came to us: to bring life out of death. Often times when we experience tragedy we tend to react like the woman in the first reading, thinking that God has caused it as a punishment for something we have done. But the Scriptures keep telling us God causes life; God brings salvation; this is why Christ came.

I think the Scriptures invite us today to reflect on the words: "God has visited his people". In what ways have we seen this happen? 1) Has the power of God's word in Scripture ever spoken words of life to us? Have we ever given this word chance or taken the time to let it have any power in our life? Has the Lord ever spoken words of life to us through friends, or through the inner voice of the Spirit? Are we ever aware that God visits us through the power of the word? 2) Do the poor and helpless draw the kind of compassion out of us that Jesus showed? If we have cared for those in need then God has visited his people through us. 3) Have we experienced moments of fear, not a fear that wants to make us run, but an awe that makes us want to praise? Those moments may happen in prayer, in the Eucharist, in seeing the goodness of others or even the goodness in ourselves, in the birth of a child, in the love of a friend. Do we ever see any special moments as moments when God is visiting us? They happen often, if we let ourselves be sensitive to them. Recently I heard someone's confession and it was a wonderful moment of grace for this person and I felt so moved by the presence of the Lord that I almost wept as I prayed with them. God has visited his people. Do we know it when it happens? 4) Have we ever found ourselves so desperately lost and turned to the Lord only to find he was right there telling us "Do not cry." I know many people who have experienced this as true.

The Lord works so many miracles, so often though they are not the dramatic ones like in today's Gospel, before a big crowd. So often they take place within a person's heart, with no one to witness except the person themselves. And they are always miracles of life, miracles of hope, peace, grace, comfort or care. The Lord has visited his people. Do we recognize his presence with us? Do we recognize his presence now?

# 11th Sunday in Ordinary Time
## June 13, 2010

**INTRODUCTION** – (2 Samuel 12:7-10, 13; Galatians 2:16, 19-21; Luke 7:36 - 8:3) King David was a great king and loved God, but he was not perfect. Today's reading occurs shortly after he sinned seriously with Bathsheba and then arranged for her husband, Uriah, to be killed in battle. Nathan, God's prophet at the time, was given the mission of confronting the king. The word "Lord" as used in today's reading refers to God mostly, but "lord" also refers to David's predecessor, King Saul, when God tells David that God had given him his lord's house and wives.

**HOMILY** – I have a rather brief homily so Sister Joan (our mission spokesperson) can have some time to talk at the end of Mass. There are several themes in today's liturgy, but the one that predominates is God's forgiveness. God forgave David when he repented. Jesus forgave the sinful woman. We don't know when or under what circumstances he did; perhaps she was inspired by one of his parables or teachings. But the gist of Jesus' parable is that having been forgiven, she was immensely grateful. (By the way, this scene is pictured in the stained glass window above the side door on the Pitt Street side of the Church.) When Jesus told her: "Your sins are forgiven," he was giving her concrete assurance of the forgiveness she had received, just as the words of the priest in the sacrament of penance gives us that assurance.

Many years ago a couple came to me with marriage problems. I do not remember all the details any longer, but the husband had a long list of his wife's faults. She was a good-hearted person and was willing to work on the things that bothered him, but he couldn't forgive anything she did wrong. I suggested to him that she must have forgiven him of some of his faults and that he should do the same for her. I was left speechless when he told me, "I don't have any faults." Not surprisingly, the marriage didn't survive. Simon, the Pharisee in today's gospel reminds me of that man. No wonder he showed such little love. He saw himself as perfect. The sinful woman was aware of her past sins, but she knew she had been forgiven and she knew Jesus was instrumental in her receiving forgiveness.

The message Jesus spoke as he began his ministry of preaching and healing was "The time has come! The kingdom of God is near! Turn from your sins and believe this Good News!" No matter how bad we've been, if we're sorry and change our ways, God's mercy is there for us for God's mercy is always greater than our sins. Knowing this should bring us to greater love for God. If we think we're perfect, we need to take a more honest look at ourselves in the light of the gospel. Do we come before God today as in need of his mercy and grateful for it, or do we come before God like the Pharisee in today's gospel?

# 12th Sunday in Ordinary Time
## June 20, 2010

INTRODUCTION – (Zechariah 12:10-11, 13:1; Galatians 3:26-29; Luke 9:18-24) "Christ" was not Jesus' second name. The word Christ (or Christos in Greek meant the "Anointed One." In Hebrew the word for the "Anointed One" was Messiah). In all of Jewish literature before the time of Jesus, there was never a hint that the Christ would suffer and die. The Jewish view was that the Christ would be a powerful and gifted king or a cosmic judge of the earth or a great high priest who would authentically teach God's word. As God's Anointed One, the Christ would liberate God's people and save them from the Roman occupation. In today's gospel Peter acknowledges Jesus was the Christ of God. But when Jesus predicted his suffering, his rejection and his death, it was as if Jesus was speaking in Chinese. It was totally beyond the Apostles' ability to comprehend. We can see in Jewish history and in the Old Testament that there were many holy people who suffered and were put to death such as the prophets or kings or Jewish martyrs, but the idea of suffering and death was never mentioned in relation to the Christ. Today's first reading from Zechariah foretells a time when God would purify his people and his people would deeply repent over one of God's servants whom they had killed. Jerusalem's mourning and repentance would lead to their purification. The person Zechariah was speaking of has never been identified, but after the resurrection, Jesus' followers could look back into the Old Testament. There they found a deeper meaning in such passages as referring to the sufferings of Christ, the Messiah. St. John's gospel specifically applies today's first reading to Jesus' being pierced by a lance as he hung on the cross.

"They shall look on him whom they have pierced." (Jn 19:37).

**HOMILY** – I wish all of our fathers today a very happy father's day. A devoted father used to pray with his children and sing to them before they went to sleep – but he quit singing one evening when he heard his five year old tell his three year old "if you pretend you're asleep he'll quit singing." Devotion doesn't get much respect these days. Anyway thanks to all our fathers for their devotion and dedication. (This joke has nothing to do with Mass. I love to hear all of you sing.)

Today's gospel reminded me of the old joke when the Holy Father one day was visiting the local hospital which he would do on special occasions. By accident he got on the psych floor and walked into the room of an old man who gave him little recognition. Even as the pope tried to make a little conversation, the man ignored him. Finally the pope asked, "Do you know who I am?" The old man said "no, but if you ask the nurse at the desk, she'll tell you who you are."

When Jesus asked his Apostles: "Who do you say that I am?" it wasn't because he didn't know himself who he was. He was definitely aware who he was. His actions showed that awareness as he taught with authority, healed the sick, cast out demons, forgave sins, quieted a storm, walked on water or fed thousands of people with five barley loaves and a couple of fish. The gospels picture him as a person who is convinced he can speak and act for God, with a power that went beyond ordinary human experience. Jesus knew who he was. In today's gospel he was trying to find out if the disciples were beginning to discover who he was, if they were beginning to understand some of the things he had been trying to teach them. From the way Peter answered, it showed he was learning, but he was just at the beginning stage. So Jesus strongly insisted they not tell anyone. They had much to learn before they could start teaching others. If the Apostles couldn't understand the part about suffering and death, no one else would either, for, as I said earlier, no teaching or writing before Christ had ever connected the Christ (the Messiah) with having to suffer and die. In everyone's thinking, the Messiah would be great and powerful and victorious over all the enemies of the Jews. Jesus saw it all differently. We can't fault the Apostles for their limited understanding; all of us struggle to understand suffering, especially why good people suffer.

Then Jesus added another thought. He knew that those who would follow him would sometimes have to risk their lives in order to be his follower. That is still true today – fortunately though not in our country at this time in history. The greatest suffering or sacrifice most of us have to deal with as followers of Christ is to keep the Commandments and to give up one hour a week to go to Mass – and many find even that too hard. What would we do if we were threatened with arrest, or confiscation of our property, or even death because we are Christians or Catholics? That's scary and none of us like to think of such things. Although there is a greater or lesser amount of sacrifice involved in following Jesus, we are guaranteed by Jesus' own words, by his resurrection, and by his gift of himself to us daily or weekly in the Eucharist that he is our savior, that he will not abandon us if we do not abandon him, and that the blessings he has prepared for us far outweigh any sacrifices we have to make in order to remain faithful to him. Amen.

# 13th Sunday in Ordinary Time
## July 1, 2007

**INTRODUCTION** – (1 Kgs 19:16b, 19-21; Gal 5:1, 13-18; Luke 9:51-62) Today's gospel reading brings us to a critical point in St. Luke's gospel. St. Luke tells us at this point in his gospel that Jesus turned his face toward Jerusalem. From this point on in Luke, everything that Jesus said or did took place while he was on his way to Jerusalem. This part of Luke's gospel is referred to as the "Journey narrative." When Jesus decided to go to Jerusalem, he knew what was ahead for him, nonetheless, he started his journey with courage and determination. He warns those who would follow him that following him would require sacrifice, and there wasn't time for second thoughts or to be indecisive.

Our first reading may seem to be a strange one, but it was chosen to correspond with the idea of total commitment to one's call. It tells about two Old Testament prophets, Elijah and Elisha. Elijah is getting old and his life is coming to an end. At God's command he chooses Elisha to replace him. Placing his mantle on Elisha's shoulders symbolized this call. Having 12 yoke of oxen to plow with would indicate that Elisha must have been a prosperous farmer. His sacrificing the animals and burning his equipment indicates a total commitment to his vocation. He broke completely with his former way of life and did not look back.

**HOMILY** – The gospels have one objective, to lead us to Christ. Christ has one objective, to lead us to God. And God has one objective, to bring us to eternal happiness. Today's gospel, in its desire to lead us to Christ does not picture Christ as "an easy going, do whatever you want, you're all going to get to heaven anyway" kind of person. Jesus is the most loving person who ever lived, and at the same time, when it comes to eternal life, he is a non wishy-washy, ambivalent person. With regard to salvation he is no nonsense. Some people might even consider his words hard.

Let us consider some of these hard sayings. We hear first of all about an encounter with the Samaritans. Most of us probably think of the Samaritans as nice people, because of the parable of the good Samaritan. But there was considerable animosity between the Jews and the Samaritans. A Jew could risk his life traveling through Samaria and as we see in today's gospel, Jesus is prudently sending messengers ahead of him to see if a particular town would receive him. They wouldn't. James and John were all for calling down destruction upon that town. Not only did they want bad to happen to those people, they wanted to be involved. They asked Jesus, "Do you want us to call down fire from heaven upon them?" Jesus just rebuked them and moved on. Jesus did not come to condemn but to save. He was a man of peace. You are possibly thinking, how is what Jesus said here a hard saying? Well, consider who are the Samaritans in your life, the people you would like to get rid of if you could? Can you have the same attitude as Jesus, willing to avoid vengeance, willing to forgive, looking for ways to find peace? It's not always easy.

The other two or three sayings are hard ones too. There is someone in the gospel who comes up to Jesus and wants to follow him. Jesus describes the sacrifices that might be involved, especially the sacrifice of not even having a place to call home. Those who lived in the early Church had many sacrifices to make to stay faithful to our Lord, even to the extent of maybe having to sacrifice their lives. People still do in other places of the world today. But in our country so many people find it hard to sacrifice an hour for Sunday Mass or time to pray during the week, not to mention the sacrifice involved in keeping the commandments. Being a Christian is not just a matter of saying we are. It is living the way Christ wants us to.

"Let the dead bury their dead" is one of the hardest to understand. I have always understood this as the situation of the young man who wouldn't be ready to follow Jesus until his father died which may have been years away. Jesus was saying there wouldn't be time. How many times do we say when I get this done or that done, then I'll begin going to Church more or spend more time praying? We're all busy today. Where we choose to spend our time tells us what's important to us. The devil's biggest temptation for many of us is to tell us "you have lots of time. You can pray later. You can do that good deed later. Just relax for a little while. You owe it to yourself." (Of course we need to relax at times, but we also need to make time for the Lord.)

The last statement is very similar. "No one who sets a hand to the plow and looks to what was left behind is fit for the kingdom of God." Our following Christ has to be serious. We can't be indecisive and uncommitted. We can't let feelings alone guide us, deciding to pray when we feel like it and putting our faith aside when we don't feel like it. Our faith is too important for that. I remember all the new faces I saw in church after 9/11. I'm glad people came but for many the enthusiasm didn't last. God deserves better than a passing thought or a spurt of piety when we happen to feel like it.

Hard sayings! They sure are. Are they meant to accuse us or put us down or depress us? No. Our Lord's words to us come from his love and his objective is to lead us to holiness and eternal happiness.

# 14th Sunday in Ordinary Time
## July 8, 2007

**INTRODUCTION** – (Isa 66:10-14c; Gal 6:14-18; Luke 10:1-12, 17-20) Our first reading describes a time in Jewish history right after the Babylonian exile. The Jews had been returning home to Israel after they had been slaves and exiles for 50 years. Their cities, lands and homes were in ruins. Consequently, they were discouraged and depressed. God encouraged them with messages of comfort and hope through the prophet Isaiah. He did not bring them home from exile to abandon them. Jerusalem will be like a mother once again, nurturing them and caring for them. They must rejoice. They will enjoy prosperity once again. The psalm refrain echoes this call to rejoice.

**HOMILY** – Only St. Luke tells us of the 72 disciples Jesus sent out. There was too much to do for the Twelve. Even today, the official leaders of the Church cannot reach all the people who need to hear God's message of love and peace. For Jesus it was quite a few more helpers he had to recruit. It seems the first thing he said to them was "there aren't even enough of you." "The harvest is abundant but the laborers are few; pray for more workers for the harvest." The next thing he did was warn them. It would be a dangerous job. They would be like lambs in the midst of wolves. That's not a very appealing image. Lambs have no defense. Their only defense is their shepherd. Of course, Jesus knew the heavenly Father would watch over them. Jesus sent them out in pairs. He knows we need each other's support in our journey of faith. Their mission probably didn't take them very far and probably not for a very long time. That's partly why they needed no money or luggage. The other reason they needed to take nothing with them was because they needed to learn to rely on God to provide for them. They had God's peace, which they could share with whoever was open to it. They had power over demons and they had the gift to heal. You would think they would have been received with open arms wherever they went and it seems as if they were. They came back to Jesus full of joy. Their mission was urgent; they weren't to stand around shooting the breeze with people, "greet no one along the way," and their message was simple. They weren't ready to preach or teach like Jesus did. They were only to tell people the kingdom of God was near.

What is the kingdom of God? We pray for it all the time: "Thy kingdom come." Jesus preached about it many times, often in parables. It is something that not all people want to be part of for it will be like a farmer's field where some of the seed is productive while some withers and dies. Or it is like a field where wheat and weeds grow together until harvest when the wheat is kept and the weeds are destroyed. But for those who open their hearts to the kingdom, it will be wonderful. It will be like a great banquet, like the wedding celebration for a prince. It will be eternal, it will be peaceful, it will be a rule of love, it will be joy beyond our ability to imagine. Because it is near, Jesus tells his 72, "rejoice, rejoice that your names are written in heaven."

I'm going to tell you a story about what heaven might be like. Old Mr. Murphy loved Ireland. He worked and toiled on its land when he was young. He poured his sweat into its soil. He raised his sons and daughters on its fertile ground. He fought for its freedom. When he could, he traveled its length and breadth. He loved it so much that when it came time to die, he had his sons carry him outside so he could lay next to the ground. He even grabbed a handful of earth to hold onto. And that's the way he died. When he got to heaven's gates God came to meet him. God had the appearance of an old man, like we're used to thinking of God the Father, white hair and beard. God told him he was a good man and welcomed him to heaven. But God said he couldn't bring that dirt into heaven. Murphy couldn't let go of it; he loved Ireland so much. So God left Murphy standing at heaven's gate and went back inside. A few years past and God came out again, this time with the appearance of one of Murphy's drinking buddies. They chatted and told a few jokes, then God invited Murphy to come on in but to let go of the dirt he was holding onto. But Murphy couldn't; he loved Ireland so much. So God sadly left him there at heaven's gates. After more years God appeared again, this time as one of Murphy's granddaughters. She told him how everyone missed him and begged him to come in. By this time Murphy's joints had stiffened and his hands could no longer hold on to the little part of Ireland he was trying to take with him. The soil fell from his hands and God brought Murphy inside. Once inside he couldn't believe it, there before his eyes was his beloved Ireland and much more besides. Sometimes people are so enamored of the little bits and pieces of God's creation that they have a hold on that they can't believe there could be anything better. But if we open ourselves in faith to whatever God asks of us, if we open ourselves in faith to the glory that Christ promised to those who follow him, we will already begin to know God's kingdom. Then we will understand Jesus' parable that the kingdom is like a treasure buried in a field or a pearl of great price. The kingdom is something we cannot see now, but it is near for those who see it in faith. It is joy beyond imagining.

The power and presence of the risen Christ fills us when God's grace is in us, for that is what grace is: God's life. It is a life that will endure forever in peace and love. This is the good news, the gospel, this was the preaching of Jesus, the proclamation of the 72, "The Kingdom of God is near." Believe it, and in this faith and this hope, rejoice.

## 15th Sunday in Ordinary Time
### July 11, 2010

**INTRODUCTION** – (Deut 30:10-14; Colossians 1:15-20; Luke 10:25-37) The Book of Deuteronomy is a series of sermons addressed to the people of Israel by Moses right before they were to enter the Promised Land. Moses had led them from the slavery of Egypt and was with them for many years as they traveled through the Sinai desert. Moses knew he would die before the people could enter their Promised Land, so he is in a sense giving them some last words of wisdom before he would have to leave them. Today's first reading begins with an incomplete sentence: "If only you would heed the voice of the Lord" The sentence implies that God would bless them greatly "if only they would heed the voice of the Lord" The passage goes on to stress that people do not have to guess what God wants of them. God has been very clear as to how he wants us to live. It's no hidden mystery. This concept connects with today's gospel, the story of the good Samaritan. The story is depicted in our stained glass window by the ramp to the parking lot. When a scholar of the law asked Jesus what God wants of us, Jesus' reply to the man shows that the man already knew the answer to his question. Almost instinctively, we all know what God wants of all of us. Knowing it is not the problem, but living it is.

**HOMILY** – I think most of you know I've been on a tour to Rome to see our new Archbishop receive the pallium. I hear you've prayed for me and I'm grateful. Although there was an explanation of the pallium in the Catholic Telegraph, not everyone gets the Telegraph, so I would like to explain it. A pallium is a somewhat circular strip of white cloth made of lambs wool that fits over the archbishop's head with a piece of the same cloth hanging about seven inches down the front and the back. Only the pope and archbishops wear the pallium, and they wear it over their vestments when they are celebrating Mass. It is a sign that the archbishop is in union with the pope. It is made out of lamb's wool that has been blessed, and it reminds a person of the good shepherd that found the one sheep that was lost and carried it back to the sheepfold on his shoulders. The Archbishop is our chief shepherd who carries on his shoulders the spiritual responsibility for this Archdiocese.

On Monday evening, before the feast of Sts. Peter and Paul, which is a holy day and a holiday in Rome, we went to the residence of the US ambassador to the Vatican for a little reception for the three archbishops from the United States who were to receive the pallium. After the reception, we went to St. Paul's outside the Wall where the Holy Father had Evening Prayer. I was in Rome many years ago, but it was the first time I ever saw the pope in real life and not just in pictures or on TV. St. Boniface Church has many features similar to St. Paul's in Rome and while there I enjoyed noticing a number of similarities. The next day, on the feast of Sts. Peter and Paul, the Holy Father conferred the pallium on 38 archbishops at St. Peter's Basilica. I got to see the Holy Father fairly close up as he processed in. He looked very joyful and stopped to shake hands with some of the children in the church. The third time I saw him was in a general audience in St. Peter's square. We had really good seats, but to get them we had to be two hours early. A lot of people had umbrellas to protect themselves from the sun. They were told to fold up their umbrellas when the pope came in so they didn't block the view of people behind them, and they did. But when all the bishops and cardinals came in, they sat in front of us and the first thing they did was put up their umbrellas. There is a good picture of them in the Telegraph holding up their umbrellas. On the other days of the week, we got to say Mass in some important Basilicas, with the five priests on the tour concelebrating with the Archbishop. I felt honored to get to preach to the group at St. John Lateran, which is considered the cathedral of Rome, a church built originally by Constantine after he ended the persecution of Christians.

We saw a lot of other places and had a lot of other experiences I could talk about, including the visit of a classmate from seminary days who took an all-night train from Venice to come to Rome so we could visit for a few hours (which meant a lot to me). But lest I bore you with more travelogue, I will switch gears here with a quotation from a sermon by St. Augustine. It was given on the occasion of the dedication of a Church (perhaps on the feast of the solemnity of the dedication of St. John Lateran which we celebrate every year in November). Augustine said, "what was done here, as these walls were rising, is reproduced when we bring together those who believe in Christ. For, by believing, they are hewn out, as it were from mountains and forests, like stones and timber. Believers are as it were shaped, squared and planed by the hands of the workers and artisans through baptism, instruction and Eucharist. Nevertheless, they do not make a house for the Lord until they are fitted together through love."

This brings us to the gospel message for today: love. It

is the basic law on which all law is built: love for God and love for one another. We are here today out of love, following Jesus' command at the Last Supper that we do this in memory of him. We show our love for God also through prayer (following the example Jesus gave us) and through keeping his commandments for he told us: "if you love me you will keep my commandments." To encourage us to love one another, in addition to the story of the Good Samaritan in Luke's gospel, he told us in Matthew's gospel: "what you do to the least of my brothers and sisters you do for me." If we need further explanation of what love is, St. Paul expresses it so beautifully in 1 Corinthians, chapter 13: love is patient, love is kind etc. This is probably the most well know part of any of the thirteen letters attributed to St. Paul. Notice when the Scriptures talk about love, they don't refer to warm, fuzzy feelings, (which may or may not occur in conjunction with love), but in talking of love, the Scriptures talk about what we do to honor God and to care for one another. Today's gospel message on love is a lifetime task. With inspiration from Jesus, who has shown us great love, and with the help of the Holy Spirit, may we continue to grow in God's love. Amen.

# 16th Sunday in Ordinary Time
## July 18, 2010

**INTRODUCTION** – (Genesis 18:1-10; Colossians 1: 24-28; Luke 10:38-42) We never know when God might surprise us and pay us a visit. Sometimes God's visits come with good ideas or with a strong awareness that we're not alone. Sometimes they come with a deep sense of peace or with a twinge of conscience. Sometimes they come when we meet a holy person or a person who is in desperate need of our help. And, of course, God comes to visit us as our life in this world reaches its end.

Our first reading is about Abraham who welcomes three strangers. It's hard to picture Abraham preparing such a lavish banquet for his guests with such energy and agility since the previous chapter had just told us Abraham was 100 years old. I have to wonder what kind of vitamins he was taking. Abraham didn't realize at first that it was God whom he was entertaining. God had come to tell him that his lifelong desire that he and his wife, Sarah, would have a son would finally be fulfilled. As God assured Abraham of this blessing, Abraham could see that their roles were reversed. Suddenly, Abraham was not the prosperous desert chieftain providing hospitality to three hungry travelers. He was simply a creature of God receiving a blessing from his Creator. Our first reading prepares us for the story of Martha and Mary (illustrated by our stained glass window) as these two sisters are visited by the One who could give them every blessing and the word of life.

HOMILY – Not so long ago I had a conversation with a friend. He has been a good Catholic all his life. We were talking about prayer. I shared with him one of the ways that I pray that has been a great support to me ever since I was a young child. I said I just imagine as if our Lord were sitting at a table with me or out walking with me and we were talking. I talk about anything that's on my mind just as if I could really see him – for I do believe he is really with me all the time. From the expression on my friend's face, I could see this was the first time an idea like that had ever crossed his mind. He said, "I don't know what I would say if our Lord showed up at my home and just wanted to visit for a little while." I said "Just talk with him like you would with anyone who is a good friend." I suggested he try it for ten minutes a day. I haven't heard how it's working with him, but I wonder how many other believers would feel comfortable praying that way. There are many other forms of prayer, of course, reading Scripture, the rosary, praying out of a prayer book, meditating on a spiritual theme, reading about the saints, holy hours before the Blessed Sacrament, praying the psalms and especially the Eucharist which is the summit of all our prayer. But this type of informal prayer, just sitting and talking things over with our Lord, or just sitting quietly in his presence has been a real blessing for me. I do it every day, whether I feel like it or not, and that's the recommendation of all spiritual writers, and it's always something good. In the original version of the gospel, in Greek, that's what Jesus said about Mary sitting at his feet: "she has chosen the good part, which shall not be taken from her."

In last week's gospel, a Jewish leader asked Jesus a question: "What must I do to inherit eternal life?" The story of the Good Samaritan about love of neighbor gave us Jesus' answer. It is quite possible that St. Luke intends today's story about Martha and Mary as a further answer to that question. The Christian life is about doing good and being good, but it is also about having a close relationship with God. "You shall love the Lord, your God, with all your heart, with all your being, with all your strength, and with all your mind and your neighbor as yourself." This was the entire answer to the question, "What must I do to inherit eternal life?"

It's obvious Martha and Mary were on very good terms with Jesus. Although Luke doesn't tell us, Martha and Mary lived in Bethany, just under two miles outside of Jerusalem. It's most likely the place where Jesus stayed when he came to Jerusalem for important feasts – for on such feasts Jerusalem was packed with visitors and lodgings were scarce. You can just imagine Jesus smiling as he says: "Martha, Martha" It is a friendly response. In telling her "one thing" is important, it does not imply that the practical necessities of life, such as eating and drinking were not important. It's more that Martha, the older sister, who wanted all her guests to be well taken card of, was troubled over too many things, too many things to take some time just to listen to our Lord and to speak with him. Martha was doing a good thing, but it was time to slow down and hear the word of life. It's hard to imagine that Mary, whom we know from John's gospel, deeply loved Jesus, would have shirked her duty and left the whole burden of being hospitable to her sister. I think Martha imagined there was a great deal more to be done than was really needed. Certainly Jesus seems to have implied as much.

The story has a lot to tell us about our busy lives today. We are to do good, but one of the good things we are to do is to slow down and hear the word of life – which we are doing at this time. So, thank you for being here today. Amen.

## 17th Sunday in Ordinary Time
### July 25, 2010

**INTRODUCTION** – (Genesis 18:20-32; Colossians 2:12-14; Luke 11:1-13) Last Sunday's first reading told us about a visit Abraham had from three strangers. Abraham provided a feast for them and as it turned out one of the three visitors was God himself. God was on his way to two cities near the Dead Sea, Sodom and Gomorrah, and he invited Abraham to go with him. On the way God took Abraham into his confidence and told him the cities were about to be destroyed because of their depravity and immorality. Notice the comfortable yet respectful familiarity that existed between God and Abraham.

HOMILY – A man was driving around downtown in a sweat because he couldn't find a parking place and he was late for an important meeting. Looking up to heaven he prayed, "Lord help me! If you find me a parking place I'll go to Mass every Sunday for the rest of my life and I'll give up drinking whiskey." Miraculously, a parking place opened up right in front of the building where he had his meeting. The man looked up to heaven again and said, "Never mind, God; I just found one."

A Catholic School teacher asked one of her young students "now tell me honestly, Johnny, do you say prayers before eating?" "No, teacher," Johnny said, "I don't have to. My mom is a good cook." Johnny hadn't learned yet that prayer is more than asking for things.

I would like to go back to the gospel from two weeks ago. A scribe asked Jesus "What must I do to inherit eternal life?" Jesus answered with a lesson on love by telling the story of the Good Samaritan. Last week was the story of Martha and Mary, where Mary sat at Jesus' feet listening to him. It is most likely St. Luke was trying to tell us it's good to help our neighbor, but it's also good to take time to be with our Lord and get away from all the ways we manage to keep busy. Remember the answer to the question, "What must I do to inherit eternal life?" has two parts. We are to love God with our whole being and love our neighbor as ourselves. Today's gospel follows immediately after the story about Martha and Mary. It seems that after telling us it is a good thing to spend time with our Lord, St. Luke is giving us an additional lesson on prayer.

We are more familiar with St. Matthew's version of the Our Father. St. Luke's version is essentially the same but a little shorter. St. Luke connects it with an encouragement to persevere in prayer and not quit. Perseverance in prayer was the point of today's first reading where Abraham kept asking God to spare the cities of Sodom and Gomorrah if he could find just a few innocent people there. Don't you wonder what God would have done if Abraham had persevered and had not stopped at the number ten but continued to bargain with God. As it was, there were four innocent people in the two cities, Lot, his wife and his two daughters and God sent an angel to lead them to safety, although Lot's wife disobeyed the angel and turned around to look.

Somehow my father had the idea that it was being selfish to pray for his own needs. I don't know where he got that idea, and I would often tell him he was wrong (something he didn't like to hear). I think the Our Father teaches us we should pray for all the things we need, including a parking place, if we need one. But the Our Father also teaches us first to praise God and to align our will with God's will before praying for ourselves.

Perseverance in prayer is one of the most important lessons we need to learn if we're going to grow spiritually. In our world today we learn to hate waiting for things. That includes waiting for God although we also know that in life we do not accomplish anything worthwhile without patience and perseverance. We know we don't need to pray in order to inform God of what we need and we don't have to wake him up or get his attention because he knows every detail of our lives (all the hairs of our heads are counted). We need to pray and to keep asking and knocking so that we can develop our relationship with our God and our creator, a relationship that is the most important relationship of all relationships, a relationship where we recognize he is Our Father who cares for us and loves us

At the end of today's gospel, Jesus said, "Ask and you **will** receive." He doesn't say, "you might receive or maybe you'll receive, but you **will** receive." What he is saying is that no prayer is wasted. Prayer **cannot** fail to bring some blessing – even if it's not the thing we think we need most. If we truly believe God is all-wise and all-loving, then we have to conclude that if we do not receive what we've asked for, God has something better in mind. Partly why people give up on prayer is they do not have this faith in God's wisdom and love. Prayer will always work for us in some marvelous way. We must trust the Lord in that. Amen.

## 18th Sunday in Ordinary Time
### August 1, 2010

**INTRODUCTION** – (Ecclesiastes 1:2; 2:21-23; Colossians 3:1-5, 9-11; Luke 12:13-21) One of the most well-known passages in the bible begins with the line: "For everything there is a season...a time for every matter under heaven. A time to be born and a time to die, and so on...." That passage is from a book in the Old Testament that has two names: in Hebrew it is called Qoheleth; in Greek it is called Ecclesiastes. The author of the book is called Qoheleth, which simply means, "one who convenes an assembly." About all we know about the author is that he was likely a Jewish teacher or preacher. Today is the only Sunday in the three-year cycle when we read from Qoheleth. Today's short passage reminds us of the passing nature of all things, a theme we hear again in the gospel.

**HOMILY** – There was a barber who was moved by the Sunday homily to witness his faith in God with greater enthusiasm. So when his first customer came into the barber shop on Monday morning and asked for a shave, the barber invited him to take a seat in the barber chair and then asked to be excused for a moment. He went to a back room and prayed a quick prayer saying, "Lord, my first customer just came in and I want to witness my faith to him. Give me the wisdom to say the right words. Amen." He came back with a bible in one hand and a straight razor in the other and asked his customer, "Are you ready to meet your maker?" Our readings today ask us this same question.

A man who felt that he was being cheated out of his inheritance approached Jesus. Jesus knew his job was about something of much greater importance than a few gold or silver coins. Jesus came to announce that God is inviting us to be part of God's kingdom, a kingdom that is not of this world, a kingdom that will be more wonderful than anything this world can give us. The man, and all those listening to Jesus, needed to be reminded about what is really important in life. He said to them: "a man's life does not consist in the abundance of his possessions." Do you think this is a reminder just for the wealthy? It's a reminder for everyone. Anyone might get caught in this trap of thinking that having more and more things is what makes life worthwhile. Certainly wealth keeps food on the table and a roof over our heads, and if we do not have enough to meet our own basic needs, life is miserable. That's why Jesus constantly insists that we care for the poor and the needy, so they can have their basic needs met. Certain people were even invited to give away everything they had to the poor and then to follow Christ. We might think of some of the saints, especially St. Francis whom everyone admires, but few try to imitate. St. Francis, of course, was trying to imitate Jesus, who said, "foxes have lairs and birds have nests, but the Son of Man has nowhere to lay his head." Not everyone is called to live like Francis or Jesus, but we can learn from them and follow their spirit.

In this world we have to provide for our needs and the needs of our families. That's why God gave us a brain and gave us strength to work. But we can't forget that our greatest need is God. Apparently that's what the man who had a great harvest in Jesus' parable forgot. He thought security, independence and power were his for many more years, forgetting that our greatest security is in God. Jesus said the man was a fool, for he grew rich in a way that in the end really didn't matter much. Jesus himself was on his way to Jerusalem and he knew what waited for him there, his own suffering and death, and he knew that growing rich in good works and in our love for God is what really matters,

We don't like to be reminded how fragile our life is, that it can be taken from us anytime. We like the illusion of being in control. Jesus is really doing us a favor when he reminds us that our life in this world is only temporary, and eternity is forever. Jesus is doing us a favor reminding us of this because he's keeping us in reality. The things of this world are only of secondary importance and we must use them as the way to him and not allow them to be central in our life. St. Paul, in today's second reading, calls greed "idolatry" for greed makes wealth our primary goal in life and for wealth we set aside the goal for which we were created – which is God.

I thank you for coming today. Your being here is an indication that you are aware that God must be central in our lives. You've heard this story before, but it's worth repeating and will make a good conclusion to my homily. An American tourist, traveling in Europe, visited a wise and famous rabbi who lived there. The American was surprised when he saw how simply the man lived – in a single room with a table and chair and a number of books. "Rabbi! Where is your furniture?" asked the tourist. "Well, where is yours?" the rabbi asked. The American tourist answered, "My furniture? I'm just passing through here." The wise rabbi responded: "Although I've lived here my entire life, so am I!"

# 19th Sunday in Ordinary Time
## August 8, 2010

**INTRODUCTION** – (Wisdom 18:6-9; Hebrews 11:1-2, 8-19; Luke 12:32-48) Faith is our theme. Our second reading today has us reflect on the faith of Abraham and Sarah. Our brief first reading from the Book of Wisdom poetically expresses praise for the faith of God's people in Egypt. Following the directions Moses gave them, they prepared to leave Egypt behind and head out for the Promised Land. Our faith in Christ expresses itself in many ways. Today's gospel stresses living a good life and being ready for the Lord when he comes again.

**HOMILY** – A mother had a fidgety little boy with her in church. During the homily she leaned over and whispered something in his ear and he was good as gold the rest of the Mass. After Mass the priest asked her what she said. She said "If you don't behave, father will lose his place and he will have to start the sermon all over again." I'm sure no one gets fidgety when I preach.

One of the themes Jesus spent so much time and energy preaching about was the theme of the kingdom of God or the kingdom of heaven. A little historical background will help us understand why the concept of "kingdom" took on such major importance in the hearts and minds of God's people. From 1000 BC to 600 BC, the Jews had a king and a kingdom of their own. Actually it was not their own, but it was God's kingdom, where God was their provider, their protector and their ruler. The king ruled as God's representative. Unfortunately, many kings grossly ignored God's rules and did not lead the people in the ways of God. About 600 BC the Babylonians invaded, plundered, destroyed, enslaved and took control. The Persians (modern day

Iran) controlled Israel after they conquered the Babylonians, then Alexander the Great (from Greece) conquered the Persians, and the Greeks controlled all the land from Greece and Egypt to India. The Jews successfully regained their autonomy shortly before the time of Jesus through the Maccabean revolt. Then in 63 BC, Pompey and the Romans conquered the Jews and they were in control for over 500 years. So, at the time of Jesus, Roman rulers governed the land and, with the backing of Roman soldiers, they kept order and made sure taxes were collected for Rome. Paying taxes to a foreign government for the privilege of living in the land God had given them was especially blasphemous to the Jews. This short history might help you understand the Jewish people's desire for freedom and independence at the time of Jesus. Many people believed that God would rescue them from their suffering and from the forces of evil that were in charge. God would punish their enemies and would initiate a utopian era to be enjoyed by God's faithful people. God's kingdom would bring freedom and an end to poverty, suffering, sickness, war and hostilities. John the Baptist proclaimed that he was sent to prepare people for the coming kingdom by calling them to conversion and to a baptism of repentance. His message was: "Repent, for the kingdom of heaven is at hand!" (Mt. 3:2) His message was stern and brought many people back to God, and we know how he was beheaded by the tetrarch Herod Antipas for his efforts at reform. Jesus showed his support for John's message and mission by being baptized by John. When Jesus began his own ministry, he and his disciples (several of whom had been disciples of the Baptist) began by baptizing. Like John, Jesus taught that those who were not part of God's kingdom would suffer, but Jesus emphasized even more the unimaginable joy the kingdom would bring to those who belonged to it. He was not afraid to teach people they must live good lives if they wish to belong to God's kingdom. Jesus pictured the kingdom of God in a variety of ways, especially through his parables, his miracles and through reaching out to sinners. If we really want to understand the gospels and to know Jesus' message, we need to understand this concept of the kingdom.

In today's gospel Jesus teaches us to be ready for the kingdom. The people of Jesus' day expected it soon. The earliest Christians expected it soon. Certain groups throughout the centuries have pinpointed the exact day and time it would take place. But Jesus told us clearly no one knows when it will be, so we must always be ready. We don't want to be left out.

Jesus uses two examples: a master who had servants (who most likely were slaves) went to a wedding celebration. Jesus used a wedding celebration as an example, because no one knew when it would end – sometimes not for days. It probably depended on how long the supply of wine lasted (and whether Jesus was there to make more). In that culture a master would never be a table waiter for his servants. What Jesus is telling us by this image is that those who are ready for the kingdom will be blessed beyond their wildest expectations. The second example of a thief also dwells on the idea of uncertainty. No one knows when a thief might come so we must always be prepared.

Almost everything Jesus said and did points to the kingdom. Thus so much more could be said about this central theme of the gospels. I hope maybe, with the few ideas I did offer, we understand a little better what we pray for when we pray: "Thy kingdom come."

# Feast of the Assumption
## August 14, 2010

**INTRODUCTION:** People often confuse the Ascension and the Assumption. The Ascension commemorates Jesus ascending into heaven and taking his place at the right hand of God. It is celebrated on the Seventh Sunday of Easter. The Assumption commemorates our belief that Mary, after her life on this earth had come to an end, was raised up to eternal life and was taken into heaven, body and soul. It was only fitting that she who was Jesus' mother and who was full of grace her entire life, should share first, before all others, in the risen glory of her Son. The dogma of the Assumption was declared by Pope Pius XII in 1950, but it had been believed and celebrated for centuries before that.

**Vigil Mass:** Our first reading (1 Chronicles 15:3-4, 15-16; 16:1-2) is about the Ark of the Covenant, the sacred gold-plated box that contained the Ten Commandments. The Ark was the unique symbol of God's presence with Israel. It was constructed in the desert by Moses on the way to the Promised Land. When King David established his capital in Jerusalem about the year 1000 BC, he brought the Ark there. Today's reading describes this solemn and joyful occasion. In Christian symbolism, Mary is sometimes referred to as the Ark of the Covenant. Just as God was present in a special way wherever the Ark was taken, so God was present with Mary in a most special way when she carried within her womb the only Son of God, Jesus our Savior. The early Christians also saw Jerusalem as a symbol of heaven. That symbolism is reflected in today's first reading. The Ark being taken up to Jerusalem symbolizes Mary being taken body and soul into the heavenly kingdom.

**Mass during the day:** Our first reading is from the book of Revelation. The book of Revelation is highly symbolic. Some of the symbolism is quite obvious while it requires a fairly extensive knowledge of Scripture to interpret some of the other symbols. In today's first reading we hear about a woman, a child and a dragon. The dragon represents the devil and the powers of evil at work in the world. The child is Christ. The woman in our reading has a double symbolism. She stands for Mary, the physical mother of Jesus Christ, and she stands for the Church, our spiritual mother who brings Jesus Christ to birth in us through faith and the sacraments. In today's passage the woman is rescued from the powers of the dragon and is described in great glory. This too has a double symbolism. It symbolizes the glory of Mary in the assumption. It also symbolizes God's faithful people whom he will rescue from evil and will bring, in the resurrection from the dead, into the glory of heaven.

**HOMILY** – Mary's assumption into heavenly glory is not explicitly described in the Scriptures. As St. John says at the end of his gospel, the Scriptures do not tell us everything that could be said about Jesus, what he said or did, much less does it tell us everything about Mary or the Apostles or the early Church. The Church has believed for centuries that Mary was so honored in the assumption because no one followed Christ as perfectly as she did, thus it is perfectly appropriate that Mary would follow him into eternal glory, body and soul.

A painting by Raphael (Vatican Pinacoteca: Crowning of the Virgin – Oddi Altarpice) recalls the legend that when Mary's life came to an end, the apostles buried her. Thomas, however, was not there at the time and when he returned he wanted to see for himself that she had died. When they opened her tomb, her body was gone. It had been raised and was taken to heaven by her Son who crowned her as queen. St. Francis de Sales said: "What son would not bring his mother back to life and would not bring her into paradise after her death if he could?" Actually, no one knows where Mary might have passed away – whether it was in Jerusalem or in Ephesus.

Another painting by Raphael (Vatican Pinacoteca: Madonna of Foligno) is one I thought was very lovely. It is part of a larger piece which includes St. John the Baptist and St. Francis on the left and St. Jerome introducing the kneeling Sigismondo Conti who was the patron who commissioned the painting.

**Homily ending at Vigil Mass:** We celebrate the honor and privilege given to Mary. Today, in Mary, we also celebrate our hope of final glorification when Christ will raise up to new life all those who have followed him faithfully. In the gospel a woman from the crowd called Mary blessed, but Jesus reminds us why she was truly blessed, in that she "heard God's word and obeyed it."

**Homily ending at Mass during the day:** Mary praised God in her visit to Elizabeth: "The Almighty has done great things for me, and holy is his name." Today we celebrate the honor and privilege given to Mary, but today in Mary we also celebrate our hope of final glorification when Christ will raise up to new life all those who have followed him faithfully. As St. Paul tells us in his wonderful chapter on the resurrection: "For just as in Adam all die, so too in Christ shall all be brought to life but each one in proper order: Christ the first fruits; then, at his coming, those who belong to Christ." No one belonged to Christ as perfectly as Mary did. Amen.

## 20th Sunday in Ordinary Time
### August 19, 2007

**INTRODUCTION** – (Jer 38:4-6, 8-10; Heb 12:1-4; Luke 12:49-53) Unfortunately suffering and turmoil have been part of everyday life in the Middle East for a long time. Our first reading takes us back 600 years before Christ when the land we now know as Iraq had the name Babylon. The Babylonians were in power at that time in history and the king and his army's ambitions were to conquer all the nations around them. The events in our first reading occurred at a time when the Babylonians were trying to take Jerusalem. Jeremiah, God's prophet, told the Jews it was useless for them to fight or to try to defend themselves; they should just go ahead and surrender or Jerusalem would be destroyed. Such talk was viewed as unpatriotic and Jeremiah was considered a traitor. Many of the Jewish leaders decided to kill Jeremiah and they persuaded their king, Zedekiah, to give in to their wishes. He allowed Jeremiah to be thrown into a cistern to die. Later, Ebed-Melech, a Cushite (which means an Ethiopian), one of Jeremiah's friends, persuaded the king to change his mind.

**HOMILY** – – A "Calvin and Hobbes" cartoon pictured Calvin, the little boy sitting under a sign that read "kick in the butt for one dollar!" When Hobbes, a talking tiger and Calvin's playmate, saw his friend sitting under this sign, he asked "How's business?" "Awful!" Calvin replied, "and I don't know why, because so many people need a good kick in the butt!"

A lot of us might need it at times, but few of us appreciate it. The people who heard Jeremiah's predictions that Jerusalem would be destroyed if they didn't surrender weren't happy about what they heard. They hoped to get rid of Jeremiah as a result. Jesus too had to confront many of the people in authority in his day and we know what happened to him. Knowing how he would be rejected and would have to suffer for teaching God's message, he felt it only fair to warn his followers that they may be in for a lot of pain and suffering if they chose to follow him.

Pain and suffering, of course, comes to everyone, whether we are good, bad or indifferent. If we do not live good lives, often we have to suffer for it, but sometimes even those who are perfectly faithful to God have to suffer too, as we hear today. One of my favorite books, *The Road Less Traveled*, begins with a very profound insight. M. Scott Peck, a psychiatrist and Episcopal priest, begins his book by saying "Life is Difficult." That's not especially profound, but what I found so profound is his statement that once we accept life is difficult, it's not so difficult. It's more difficult for those who think it shouldn't be so. I had a good friend who was pushing a person in a wheelchair at his synagogue and while he was doing this he suffered a stroke. He would often cynically say to me "no good deed goes unpunished." I think at times we all feel that way, that life is not fair. I believe most of us have the unexpressed expectation that if we do what God wants, God should do what we want. Well, sometimes he does, and sometimes he doesn't, at least not right away.

A lot of times it's not the difficulties that come our way that cause us pain and suffering but the attitude we take toward them. Dr. Richard Carlson's book: *Don't Sweat the Small Stuff, and it's all small stuff*, tells the story of a journalist interviewing two bricklayers working at a construction site. The journalist asked the one man, "what are you doing?" He said, "I'm just an underpaid and overworked bricklayer wasting my time piling bricks on top of one another." He asked the other what he was doing and he said, "I'm the luckiest person in the world. I get to be a part of great and important projects. I help turn single bricks into magnificent structures." They were both right. We see in life what we want to see. If you want to find ugliness, you will find plenty of it. If you want to find fault with life you can find lots of reasons to do so. But the opposite is also true. There are times when in my ministry and in my life, I feel like the luckiest person in the world. I am grateful that I am in a position at times to be able to help people in very important ways. On the other hand, there have been moments when I felt like Jeremiah, sinking in the mud at the bottom of a well where everything looks dark and hopeless. It's only faith that gets me through. I know God will not fail us if we are faithful to him, but God does not always make things happen the way we think he should. When he doesn't make things go our way, we have to trust God has a better plan, a plan we do not yet see. The letter to the Hebrews which we heard speaks of the example of Jesus whose work and life seemed to be a great failure when he died on a cross, but now he has taken his seat at the right hand of the throne of God. The author of the letter encourages us not to grow despondent, but to keep alive in us the hope of eternal joy that God has promised to those who are faithful to him. When we take our last breath, that is what's really going to count. Amen.

## 21st Sunday in Ordinary Time
### August 22, 2010

**INTRODUCTION** – Our first reading today (Is. 66:18-21) comes from the time when the Jews were experiencing 50 years of exile and enslavement in Babylon. They had given up any hope of returning to their homeland in Judea and to the city where they worshipped their God, Jerusalem. The prophet we will now hear foresees great things for Jerusalem. He tells God's disheartened people they would once again worship in Jerusalem. Even more, some day people from foreign nations would come to worship with them. Even foreigners would be accepted as priests. God first chose the Jews as his chosen people, and it was through them that God expressed his desire that all people would be saved. Thus the Jews are our spiritual ancestors. A practical question comes up in today's gospel: how many really will be saved. Jesus reminds us sadly, many will not be. (Lk 13:22-30).

HOMILY – A man remembered this event from his younger days. He relates how his mother was a cleaning fanatic. One Saturday she gave him and his older brother the chore to clean their rooms. She was none too happy about how messy they were. She even kept watch as they cleaned and kept telling them to do a better job. Finally, the older brother, exasperated with having to keep doing the same job over until it was perfect, reached for a broom and asked his mother: "Can I use this, or are you planning on going somewhere?" The narrator didn't describe what happened next.

Sometimes parents are over-strict and sometimes over-lenient. It's hard to be perfect for any of us. We have to learn as we go along. But whatever imperfections parents have, mostly they are loving people and are trying to do a good job. The reason they try so hard is because they want us to learn how to live right, how to avoid doing things that are wrong, how we can grow to be successful in this life. Believe it or not, that's what God wants to teach us as well. Most of all he wants us to experience infinite happiness for all eternity. So our second reading today tells us "do not disdain the discipline of the Lord or lose heart when reproved by him." (Hebrews 12:5-7, 11-13) Sometimes people think that God gave us laws just to take the joy out of life. Keep holy the Lord's day, honor your parents, do not kill, do not commit adultery, do not steal, do not bear false witness, etc. God gave us rules and holds us accountable – not because he wants to take away our happiness. As a loving parent God wants happiness for us forever. He even sent his Son to teach us further so we could be part of his eternal kingdom, a kingdom where pain and suffering and even death would be done away with and we would experience only peace and love and joy. Going to the gospel for today, Luke tells us Jesus was on his way to Jerusalem, the place where his teachings would lead to his being put to death, but also the place where he would, through his death, initiate God's kingdom. Seventeen times Luke reminds us, in the course of Jesus' journey, that Jesus was on his way to Jerusalem because Jerusalem plays so much a role in Jesus' saving work.

On the way the question comes up: "Will only a few people be saved?" Jesus says clearly the kingdom is offered to all: people from all nations, the north and the south, the east and the west will be part of it. Jesus doesn't answer whether it will be few or many who will accept the offer; however, he does say many will not! This is one of those hard sayings of Jesus, one that many of us preachers want to soften or tiptoe around; to do that, however, would not be fair to the gospel or fair to those who came to hear it. Surveys tell us even many Catholics feel they can ignore many of the important things God wants of us, and yet they continue to feel assured they are going to be saved. That's directly contrary to the teachings of Jesus. Today Jesus tells us we must strive to enter through the narrow gate. The Greek word "'Agonízomai" (you can hear the word "agony" in this word) would be better translated "strain every nerve, take pains, exert yourself, to enter" Jesus is telling us we can't take salvation for granted. Just having a loose connection with our Lord will not do anything for us: for he tells us some will say "we ate and drank in your company and you taught in our streets" But as Jesus said, "So what, you didn't take what I said as the word of God and put it into practice. I don't know where you are from." Jesus tells us we have to exert ourselves to enter a narrow gate, a gate that people have to pass through one or two at a time. Perhaps Jesus means this image for those who believe that because they belong to a particular race, or a particular group or a particular religion, they feel that's a guarantee they have it made. We have to take Jesus seriously, and we have to understand there is an urgency about it. For eventually it will be too late and the door to the kingdom will be locked. Eventually we will run out of time. If we haven't done so already, we must make our decision now to be faithful to him.

Now if you go home and tell your friends I tried to scare the hell out of people today, you are right. You don't want to stand before the Lord and say no one warned us we should take our faith so seriously. And I don't want to have to stand before our Lord on the last day and have him say to me, "you didn't do a very good job of telling people what they should have been hearing from the pulpit." Amen.

## 22nd Sunday in Ordinary Time
### August 29, 2010

HOMILY – (Sirach 3:17-18, 20, 28-29; Heb 12:18-19, 22-24; Luke 14:1,7-14) A college professor and an elderly farmer find themselves sitting next to one another on a long flight. The college professor thinks himself very bright and decides to have a little fun with the elderly farmer. He suggests they play a game. The farmer is tired and politely says he would rather not and sits back to catch a few winks. The college professor persists saying the game is a lot of fun. He said, "I ask you a question and if you can't answer it you pay me $5. Then you ask me a question and if I can't answer it I'll pay you $500." This gets the farmer's attention so he agrees to play. So the professor asks, "How far away is the moon?" The farmer doesn't say a word but reaches into his pocket and pulls out a $5 bill and gives it to the professor. Then the professor says, "You ask me a question." So the farmer asked: "What goes up a hill with three legs and comes down with four?" The professor was challenged. He looked up references on his laptop, called a couple of his smart colleagues and after half an hour he gave up in frustration. Meantime the farmer was taking a little nap. The professor woke him and handed him $500. The farmer put it in his pocket and went back to sleep. The professor is going crazy not knowing the answer so he wakes the farmer up and asks: "Well, so what goes up a hill with three legs and comes down with four?" The farmer reached into his pocket, handed the professor $5 and went back to sleep.

Don't we all just love to see a person who thinks they are so superior be brought down to earth? Jesus tells a parable appropriate to his culture; such things as where people sat at a dinner table were carefully figured out depending on a person's age, public position, learning, attainments, wealth, etc. All of these conferred on a person the right to be seated in prominent places. Jesus made his parable about a wedding banquet which was even more formal than an ordinary meal. The point of the parable comes at the end. Jesus is not trying to teach good manners nor to teach people how to avoid embarrassment at an event. He is teaching what is important in order to enter the kingdom of God: "everyone who exalts himself will be humbled, and he who humbles himself will be exalted." When we're full of pride, we're full of ourselves and there's no place for God in our hearts. Remember, pride was the first sin. The devil told Eve if you eat of the forbidden fruit "You will not die. God knows that your eyes will be opened when you eat it. You will become just like God, knowing everything, both good and evil." (Gen 3:4-5) Adam and Eve thought the forbidden fruit would make them equal to their Creator. Those who will enjoy God's kingdom will not only be greatly blessed, but they will know how to be lovingly subjected to the one who is their King in the kingdom: God. Long ago, the prophet Micah preached: "You have been told what is good, and what the Lord requires of you: only to do the right and to love goodness and to walk humbly with your God." (Micah 7: 8) That's a good summary of what God wants of us. We see humility as singled out specifically as if it opens the door to every other virtue and to an honest relationship with God. Jesus gave us his own example to imitate when he said: "Learn from me for I am meek and humble of heart." (Mt. 11:29)

I want to remind you there are two kinds of pride and two kinds of humility. The first kind of pride is healthy pride, where we are honest about the gifts God has given us, perhaps good health, perhaps a good mind, perhaps many good influences as we grew up, perhaps a good education. We acknowledge these as coming from God and are grateful. St. Paul asks, "What do you possess that you have not received? And if you have received it why are you boasting as if you did not receive it?" (1 Cor. 4: 7) Healthy pride enables us to take care of ourselves, to try to dress appropriately, to develop and use our talents, to share with those less fortunate (as the second part of today's gospel tells us to do) and to recognize where all our blessings come from. Unhealthy pride (sometimes called neurotic pride) tries to convince us that we are perfect or at least much more superior in various ways than we really are. Unhealthy pride convinces us we don't need to give God much attention because we're quite capable of taking care of ourselves. It causes us to look down on others who are not quite as brilliant or talented or attractive or wealthy as we ourselves. This kind of pride can also backfire and turn itself on us. It can really bring us down when we don't live up to our exalted expectation of ourselves. The two kinds of humility correspond to these two types of pride. There is true humility where we honestly recognize our dependence on God and with honesty we know ourselves: our strengths and abilities, our weaknesses and limitations. False humility where we act humbly but like the people in today's gospel, we're waiting for someone to come along and say: "move up higher friend."

As you come to Mass today, you are showing you recognize who your Lord is, you are acknowledging he is Lord by giving God adoration and thanks and by recognizing your need for his help. Amen.

## 23rd Sunday in Ordinary Time
### September 5, 2010

INTRODUCTION – (Philemon 9-10, 12-17) To understand our second reading, I need to explain something about slavery in the Roman Empire in the first century. It was in many ways different than our experience of slavery before the Civil War. Slavery was common in the first century but slaves came from nations and peoples that Rome had conquered. Most slaves were probably white, many would have been educated and would have worked as musicians, scribes, craftsmen, teachers and even doctors. A slave might eventually be set free by his or her owner or buy their own way to freedom. Today's second reading is about a slave named Onesimus (a name which means "useful"). Onesimus escaped from his owner. The Greek word for an owner of slaves is "despota." Can you see an English word in that? Anyway, the owner was named Philemon (a name which means "loving"). By Roman law, a runaway slave could be punished by death. Onesimus had known Paul for Paul converted his master, Philemon, to Christ. So, in fear for his life, Onesimus ran to Paul, who was in prison at the time. Unlike today, where prisoners receive good care, the Romans locked a person up temporarily until a trial was held. It helps to know that in those days a prison was just a place where an accused person was held until their case was determined: whether they would be executed, sent into exile, have their property confiscated, or be set free. The Romans never considered it a punishment to lock up a criminal. Often prisoners needed friends or family to provide for their basic needs and, apparently, Onesimus did that for Paul. For Paul Onesimus lived up to his name: useful. In the process Paul converted him to Christ. Paul thus refers to Onesimus as his own child for he has led him to rebirth in Christ. Paul would have liked to keep Onesimus with him to help him, but he felt an obligation to send him back to Philemon. He didn't feel right benefiting from a gift that had not been given to him. Paul asked Philemon in the letter we hear in today's second reading to receive Onesimus back, not as property he might own, but as a brother in the Lord. Christianity transcends all of our relationships.

**HOMILY** – (Luke 14:25-33) On this holiday weekend, a few comments about work would be appropriate: Success in life according to Arnold Schwarzenegger is: "Work hard, stay focused and marry a Kennedy." Dave Barry quips: "When I hear about people making vast fortunes without doing any productive work or contributing anything to society, my reaction is, How do I get in on that?" An office supervisor had to speak to a new employee about her tardiness, that it was almost daily and was causing the other employees to complain. After a few moments, the new employee agreed it was a problem and asked: "Is there another door I could use?"

Now to today's gospel. Again Luke tells us Jesus was on his way to Jerusalem. Here he tells us Jesus was traveling with great crowds. Jesus' disciples and those others with him were anticipating major change in their world when Jesus would arrive in Jerusalem. They anticipated Jesus would free them from their Roman oppressors, and after 600 years of being subjects of some foreign king, their land would be their own and they would have their own king. Jesus, of course, would be their king and with his miraculous powers he would make life wonderful for them.

Jesus alone knew what was about to happen. So he told them, as he always spoke the truth, you can't follow me unless you take up your cross and follow me. (He would have made a poor politician.) Furthermore, unless you hate your father and mother, wife and children, brothers and sisters and even your own life you cannot be my disciple. "Hate!" That's a strong word. Actually the word used in Greek "miseo" does have a secondary meaning of "disregarding rather than giving preferential treatment." The first rule about understanding Scripture is to see a statement in its context. The context here is the entire New Testament where love of others, especially those to whom we owe the most love, is of supreme importance. St. Matthew also gave us this saying of Jesus in his gospel, but he words it this way: "Whoever loves his father or mother, brother or sister, more than me is not worthy of me." Most likely Matthew is an interpretation of what Jesus said and Luke's version (unless you "hate" your father and mother, etc?) is closer to the original statement of Jesus. I wonder if Jesus used such a strong word in order to shock us into realizing what he is asking of us. A quote from St. Gregory the Great, whose feast we just celebrated, is relevant to this saying of Jesus: "Perhaps it is not after all so difficult for a person to part with his possessions, but it is certainly most difficult for him to part with himself. To renounce what one has is a minor thing; but to renounce what one is, that is asking a lot." Jesus asks a lot. Why does he ask so much? It's all because that is the nature of love. Joy comes when two beings truly give themselves to one another (and are not merely using one another). God created us for joy – eternal joy. And God has given himself to us fully in the gift of his Son. He continues to give himself – especially in the Eucharist. He wants us to give ourselves fully to him so we can be fully happy.

Remember Jesus told us earlier in the gospel not to worry about what we are to eat and what we are to wear. God takes care of the birds of the air and the lilies in the field. Certainly he will take care of us. (Lk 12:22-34) Here he gives us two little examples of how we must calculate the cost of following him, just as a builder has to figure whether he can do the job before he begins to build or a king has to figure whether he can win a war before he gets into battle. I think the Lord would expect us to be prudent in planning ahead for any important element of our lives. After all, prudence is a virtue, and God expects us to use the brains he gave us. The Lord wants us to be wise in planning ahead for our eternal salvation. The way to arrive there safely is to follow him, for as he tells us in John's gospel, he is the way and the truth and the life. (Jn. 14:6) In other words we know we're not going to be in this world forever and we can't wait to start preparing for happiness with God until the angel of death stamps on our forehead: "Return to sender" and then sends us on our way.

We come to Mass today seeking to grow in our relationship with Christ who is the way, for this task of following him and putting him above everything else in our lives is an on-going process and with his guidance and with his help we will succeed. Heaven is the happiness of surrendering ourselves to the greatest love in the universe. Amen.

## 24th Sunday in Ordinary Time
### September 12, 2010

**INTRODUCTION** – God's forgiveness is today's theme. Our first reading (Exodus 32:7-11, 13-14) takes us back to Moses, about 1300 years before Christ. The people of Israel had just escaped from Egypt and were going through the desert of Sinai on their way to the Promised Land. God had already made a covenant with them at Mt. Sinai, choosing them as his special people and demanding in return that they honor him as their only God. When God called Moses back to the top of Mt. Sinai to speak with him again, the people got into trouble. They fashioned for themselves a golden calf and worshipped it as their God. This is where our first reading begins. God is angry with his people. Notice, in speaking to Moses, he calls them "your people." Moses intercedes for the people and "convinces" God to be forgiving. His prayer displays total unselfishness. God, of course, forgives them. In the second reading we hear St. Paul describe what a sinful person he once was and how God was merciful to him (1 Timothy 1:12-17). In today's gospel, which is the entire fifteenth chapter of St. Luke, we hear three beautiful parables on God's forgiveness (Lk. 15:1-32).

HOMILY – A teacher in the local high school was pulled over by the police just a few minutes after she left the school parking lot for having expired license plates. The officer asked to see her license and car registration. Students leaving around the same time began driving past, honking their horns, hooting, or admonishing their teacher. Finally, the officer asked if she was a teacher at the school. She admitted she was. "I think you've paid your debt to society," the officer concluded with a smile and left without giving her a ticket. Although the police have to do their job, if we're the one who got caught, we're grateful when we're shown mercy.

What if Jesus gave us a ticket every time we did something wrong, Boy! I would hate to pay all those fines! Jesus is not interested in catching us but in saving us. St. Paul tells us today, "You can depend on this as worthy of full acceptance: that Christ Jesus came into the world to save sinners."

St. Luke tells us today that Jesus was harshly criticized by the authorities for associating with sinners and even for eating with them. He responded by telling three stories. All three emphasize that God cares about each one of us and doesn't want any of us to be lost. Sometimes we get lost because we thoughtlessly wander off in the wrong direction, moving further and further away from our shepherd. Little by little, like a lamb looking for juicy clumps of grass, we suddenly wonder how we got lost. Sometimes we choose to get lost like in the story of the prodigal son. God is not going to find us if we do not want to be found. I think one of the main points in the story of the prodigal son (I think we could also call him the narcissistic son) is that he had to "come to his senses" and turn back to his father before he could discover his father's love and that his father was waiting for him all along. God gives us freedom to walk away from him, and it's in freedom that we must choose to return. Once we decide to do that, he's there waiting for us ready to forgive.

Why does God give us so much freedom? It's because love can only exist in an environment of freedom. If God forced us to love him, that would be a contradiction in terms for we would be robots – incapable of making the choice to love.

A person might say "that's all well and good, but our religion tells us we will be eternally punished if we choose not to love God or follow him." Indeed, there will be punishment, but not one God imposes on us. It is one that results from turning our back on the one thing that can fulfill us: God's offer of fantastic and everlasting love. The father in the parable didn't have to punish his wayward son. The son brought all his misery on himself, because he walked away from what could really bring him happiness and looked for happiness everywhere else.

That's why God is so ready to forgive. He wants happiness for us and he knows when we open our heart to him, that alone will bring us the happiness for which we were created.

Notice the element of joy in all three parables. God is full of joy when the lost sheep, the lost coin and the lost son are found. God is joyful in our experiencing love and union with him, which alone will bring us our greatest joy now and for all eternity. Amen.

# 25th Sunday in Ordinary Time
## September 19, 2010

**INTRODUCTION** – (Amos 8:4-7; 1 Timothy 2:1-8; Luke 16, 1-13) Seven hundred fifty years Before Christ, Israel was enjoying a time of great financial and material prosperity. But spiritually they were bankrupt. In their prosperity they lost their focus on God. The Sabbath and the new moon were days of both prayer and rest. The Israelites resented this interruption in what they considered most important in life – making money. The ephah and shekel, mentioned in our first reading, were weights used in buying and selling. They didn't use honest weights, thereby cheating both their suppliers and their customers. They even exploited their customers by mixing useless materials in with the products they wanted to sell – such as mixing chaff with the wheat. The world has changed considerably since then, but in many ways human nature seems to remain the same.

**HOMILY** – Late one night, a robber wearing a ski mask jumped into the path of a well-dressed man, stuck a gun in his side and demanded "Give me your money." Indignant, the affluent looking man said, "You can't do this. I'm a United States Congressman!" "In that case," replied the robber, "give me my money."

That's what the rich man in today's gospel wanted: his money. He had heard that his employee was taking advantage of him. Whether the employee was stealing from the rich man or not isn't the main point, although he probably was. And whether the employee reducing the debt that various business people owed his master was honest or dishonest is not the point of the parable either. The main point is that the employee was clever and wasted no time in planning for a secure future for himself.

Jesus tells us we need to be just as clever in planning for a secure future for ourselves, and it's not just for the few years we spend on this earth that we have to provide, but also for our time in eternity. Jesus is constantly reminding us that material things can make us feel so secure in this life that we forget about what is most important, our eternal life. That was the point of today's first reading from Amos. The prosperous era that the Israelites were enjoying 750 years before Christ led them to forget about the God who had blessed them so richly. When they lost touch with God, this led to the moral decline of the nation and its eventual collapse. Our life in this world is temporary. Eternity is forever. Jesus is telling us today to use the blessings God has given us to help us get closer to God and not let our possessions become a god in themselves.

## 26th Sunday in Ordinary Time
### September 26, 2010

INTRODUCTION – Today again we listen to the prophet Amos. (Amos 6:1a, 4-7) His words are directed to the Judeans, those living the southern kingdom of Israel. He addresses them as "the complacent in Zion." (Zion is another name for Jerusalem). Perhaps this warning came after the Assyrians destroyed the northern kingdom of Israel which, in today's reading, is called "Joseph." (Joseph is the name of the patriarch who was sold into slavery by his brothers and ended up being next to the pharaoh in power in Egypt. Many of his descendents had settled in the northern portion of Israel which the Assyrians destroyed.) The complacent in Jerusalem were living pampered, comfortable lives, paying no attention to the devastation of the north and not concerned that their own country was headed toward the same fate because of their social and moral depravity. Amos' words proved to be true.

**HOMILY** – (1 Timothy 6:11-16; Luke 16:19-31) The phone rang at the church office. The pastor answered: "St. Cyprian!" The caller asked: "Is this the pastor?" "Yes, it is." "This is the Internal Revenue Service. We wonder if you can help us." "I'll try." "Do you know Harold Schwartz?" "I do." "Is he a member of your congregation." "He is." Did he donate $10,000." "He will." (from *Laughter, the Best Medicine, Reader's Digest*, pg 293)

A lot of people say "money is the root of all evil" thinking they are quoting the Bible. But what the Bible actually says in 1 Tim 6:10: "the love of money is the root of all evil." Jesus never condemned the wealthy for having wealth. He condemned them for letting their wealth make them forget about the God who had blessed them so generously – like the farmer we heard about several weeks ago. He had such a great harvest that he had to tear down his barns to build bigger ones and he gave no thought to the afterlife. Or Jesus condemned the wealthy for letting their wealth lead them into dishonesty like the unjust steward we heard about last week. Or Jesus condemned the wealthy because they let their wealth turn them into selfish, self-centered persons like the rich man in today's gospel.

Today's parable would have been quite a shock for those who heard it. For in Jewish mentality, if a person was wealthy they were assumed to be good people whom God favored. If a person were poor or sick or infirmed, they were assumed to be sinners whom God was punishing for something. But things didn't work out that way for the rich man and Lazarus. It is an example of the kingdom of God that Jesus preached. Those who wish to be part of God's kingdom must love God and others. Love is the supreme law and love is not just a warm fuzzy feeling but is a willingness to even make sacrifices for others. Some people Jesus asked to give everything away and come follow him. He didn't ask that of everyone, but he did ask everyone to love God with our whole selves and to love our neighbor as we love ourselves.

What should the rich man have done? Jesus doesn't give us a specific answer. Perhaps he wants us to ask ourselves what we might have done if we were in his place. He does give us a general answer in the second part of the parable. The rich man wanted Lazarus to visit his brothers and warn them about how they should be living. Jesus said they have Moses and the prophets, that is, they have the Scriptures to guide them. If they don't pay attention to the Scriptures, they probably won't be impressed by someone who rises from the dead.

In Jesus' day, people didn't know what was going on elsewhere in the world. With the internet we know the instant an earthquake or a tsunami kills hundreds and thousands of people and leaves other thousands homeless. Knowing all this can give us guilty feelings, thinking we should help everyone – which we can't; or at least I know I can't. I try to help people in need, according to what my time and resources allow, according to their need and according to the responsibility I may have toward them. (Charity does begin at home, but it doesn't stay there.) Although I can't help everyone, I can help some, and if we all tried to do what we could, perhaps we would be a lot more peaceful with ourselves, and the world would be a lot more loving. We come to the Eucharist today to remember where our blessings come from and to offer thanks, and we ask God's help for the days ahead when we might be in need. Amen.

# 27th Sunday in Ordinary Time
## October 3, 2010

**INTRODUCTION** – (Habakkuk 1:2-3, 2:2-4; Lk 17:5-10) Six hundred years before Christ, the Babylonians were the dominant power in the Middle East with their capital very near modern day Baghdad. The prophet Habakkuk, who speaks to us in today's first reading, lived during the very difficult period that began with the Babylonian army's first assault against the Holy Land in 604 BC, its capture of Jerusalem and its enslavement and exportation of many of the people to Babylon in 597 BC, and the eventual total destruction of Jerusalem and the Temple ten years after that. Habakkuk asks God for relief. God assures him it will come if the people just put their trust in God. God even gave detailed instructions to the king through the prophet Jeremiah on how they could avoid disaster, but the king did just the opposite. As a consequence they suffered greatly under the Babylonians.

**HOMILY** – Sister Barbara was sitting by the window of her second floor convent apartment one evening, opening her mail. She received a letter from home and with it there was a $100 bill. Just as she finished reading the letter she glanced out the window and saw a shabbily dressed man down by the street leaning on the lamppost. He looked like he needed money more than she did, so she wrote on a piece of paper "Don't despair. Sister Barbara," wrapped the $100 bill in the note and, getting his attention, she threw it down to him. He picked it up, read it and hurriedly walked away. The next day Sister Barbara was told there was a man at the door wanting to see her. When she went to the door there was the same man waiting for her. Without a word he handed her a wad of $100 bills. "What's this," she asked. "That's the

$8,000 you have coming Sister," he replied. "Don't Despair came in first and paid 80 to 1." (from *Laughter, the Best Medicine, Reader's Digest,* pg 294)

Don't despair seems to fit today's theme. You can certainly hear despair in today's first reading as Habakkuk prays: "How long, O Lord? I cry for help but you do not listen!" He is having quite a struggle with God. He goes on for several more verses telling God about all the things that are happening to the Jewish people. Not only were the Babylonians defeating every nation from the Persian Gulf to the Mediterranean Sea, but God's own people in Judea and Jerusalem had turned from their worship of God to idolatry, child sacrifice and disregard for the poor and disadvantaged. Habakkuk exclaims: "I cry out to you, 'Violence!' but you do not intervene." "Why, Lord? Why?"

God's answer (as always) is "trust, have faith, be patient." God's salvation will come when God thinks it's the right time. God will not disappoint. Writing it down especially on tablets of stone or clay, would symbolize permanence. Those struggling with faith need this reassurance for "The just one, because of his faith, shall live." St. Paul quotes this line twice in his letters and it applies to faith in Christ. (Rom 1:17 and Gal 3:11). Despair won't help anyone, only faith.

It took many years until, "in the fullness of time" (Galatians 4:4), God himself appeared as the savior, not just for the Jewish people but for all people. He began his saving work when he came to live among us, but he has not finished it. So we continue to need faith until God's kingdom of eternal peace has been fully established. The apostles did have a sense that what Jesus was asking of them would require a lot of faith. In today's gospel we hear them asking Jesus to increase their faith.

It's interesting the way Jesus responds. It's like he's

telling them "Duh! What do you think I've been trying to do ever since you've known me?" (To help you increase your faith). He tells them, "even with a tiny spec of faith you could do unbelievable things." It sounds as if our Lord is saying that if they were to be tested on their faith they would probably get an F minus. What are they to do? What can we do to help our faith along?

The little lesson at the end of the gospel where we are told to do what we are expected to do is a little lesson in humility and also a little lesson in faith insofar as the only way we can increase our faith is to live it (taking time to pray, read the Scriptures and, as we are doing now, by coming to Mass). If we don't live it, it will be like muscles we don't use and will atrophy. I see it happen to people so many times. Another thing we can do is what we hear in today's second reading: "Take as your norm (your practice) the sound words that you heard from me.." (2 Timothy 1:13) Words are so important, especially the things we tell ourselves. A whole area of counseling has developed around this idea of how what we tell ourselves affects our mood. It's called cognitive therapy. What we tell ourselves also affects our faith. If we always tell ourselves negative things such as "God doesn't love me, he's too busy for me; I'm such a sinner, God can't forgive me; God doesn't hear my prayers; God isn't here when I come to Church," we are going to believe those things. We should tell ourselves what we hear from the Scriptures: "God does love me; Christ died for me; Christ hears me when I pray, even when he says 'no;' Christ truly comes to me in the Eucharist, etc." Telling ourselves those things, especially when we don't feel it, or when the devil whispers doubts in our ears, helps strengthen our faith. Jesus tells us with faith as small as a mustard seed we can do amazing things. Amen.

# 28th Sunday Ordinary Time
## October 10, 2010

**INTRODUCTION** – (2 Kings 5:14-17; 2 Timothy 2: 8-13; Luke 17:11-19) Israel and Syria (which is north of Israel and Jordan) have been fighting with each other for centuries. Today's first reading takes us back to 850 BC. They were at war then. At that time Syria was called Aram. Our reading is about an Aramean army general named Naaman. He had the dreaded disease of leprosy. His wife had an Israelite girl who was her slave. This slave was most probably captured in battle. She told her master, Naaman, about a prophet in Israel who would be able to cure his disease. That prophet was Elisha. It must have taken a lot of humility and faith for this proud Aramean general to go into enemy territory (Israel) to look for Elisha. When he located him, Elisha wouldn't even give Naaman the courtesy of coming out of his cave or hut to meet with him. He just told him through a messenger to go and bathe in the Jordan River seven times. This, too, was offensive as Naaman considered the rivers in his own country far superior to the Jordan. Naaman was insulted and decided to go back home, but his friends persuaded him to do as the prophet said. Thus our first reading begins. The reading prepares us for the gospel when we hear about Jesus healing 10 people who had leprosy.

**HOMILY** – A nurse who worked for an orthopedic surgeon tells this story. The doctor was moving to a new office across town and she and the receptionist were helping him move all his equipment. Among the items she was transporting was the skeleton the doctor used when he wanted to point out a problem area to a patient. She put the skeleton in the front seat of her car, with its bony arm stretched across the back of the drivers seat.

She hadn't thought how this might look to other drivers on the road. As she waited at a red light, the people in the car next to her really stared her down and she explained, "I'm delivering him to my doctor's office." The other driver leaned out his window and shouted: "I hate to tell you this lady, but I think its too late." (from *Laughter, the Best Medicine, Reader's Digest,* pg 203) It's nowhere recorded in the Scriptures that Jesus raised a skeleton back to life, but he did raise three others who died back to life: the daughter of Jairus, the son of the widow of Naim, and his friend Lazarus in Bethany. In a figurative way he restored life to the ten lepers whom he met on his way to Jerusalem.

Leprosy in that culture included any number of skin diseases, some of which may have been fatal, some of which may have just been a nuisance, but without proper diagnosis and medication, everyone who was thought to have leprosy was ostracized. They could no longer live among their family and friends, but had to live apart lest they infect others. They could not come to synagogue or Temple, they could not work but had to beg, they had to warn anyone coming near to them to stay away. When Jesus sent them off to the priests, he showed his intention to heal them. They wouldn't be seeing the priests for any other reason other than that the priests would declare that they were healthy. They could live a normal life again. As Son of God, whatever Jesus said, took place. Whether it was healing the sick or calming a storm. This is simply why we believe that when he said, "This is my body, this is my blood," the bread and wine truly become his body and blood. Jesus continues his healing power through the Church. He gave us a sacrament to help us in our sickness, one of the seven sacraments. Of course, we can pray on our own for good health, and we should, but the sacraments give additional power to our prayers.

The sacrament used to be called Extreme Unction because in the Middle Ages, people forgot why it was originally given to us. Vatican II restored the sacrament to its original purpose and it is now called the Anointing of the Sick. It infallibly gives us grace and help in our illness and sometimes even brings physical healing. I have seen it happen. I administer this sacrament to everyone I visit in the hospital. I always carry the holy oil with me on Sundays because many times people ask me to anoint them after Mass. I like to administer it occasionally throughout the year to everyone who wishes to receive it, and I haven't done that for a while, so I'll do it today after Mass. When we ask in faith, great things can happen, although we may have to keep on asking for a while. This is one of the ways Jesus taught us to pray – to keep on asking. I don't think we see the miracles that could occur because too often people quit praying when they don't get immediate results.

There is another very important lesson in today's gospel that I have to comment on before I end my homily: gratitude. Only one man returned to Jesus to thank him and to give glory to God. Our society is becoming more and more like this scene, when fewer and fewer come to the Eucharist (which means Thanksgiving) every week to give thanks to God. Certainly we can give thanks in our daily prayers, but there is no more perfect a way to acknowledge God's goodness to us and to thank him than the Eucharist. It is the most perfect prayer for it is a prayer through which our prayers are joined with Christ's perfect sacrifice of love. It is the prayer Jesus gave us at the Last Supper and which he asked us to pray when he said, "Do this in memory of me." So we now thank God for his goodness to us and ask him to bless us in whatever ways we need his help.

# 29th Sunday in Ordinary Time
## October 17, 2010

**INTRODUCTION** – (Exodus 17:8-13; 2 Timothy 3:14 - 4:2; Luke 18:1-8) As Moses led God's people from slavery in Egypt, through the desert, to the Promised Land, they encountered numerous threats to their lives: the army of Pharaoh, the Reed Sea they had to cross, the lack of water and food in the desert. One such threat was opposition from those peoples whose lands they had to pass through to get where they were going. Today's reading speaks of an attack by Amalek, a desert tribe living south of the Dead Sea. Moses positioned himself on a nearby hill to pray for success in battle. He prayed with his arms held high in petition. As long as he prayed, his prayer was powerful and effective. This story is an encouragement to us to persevere in our prayer, which is also the lesson in today's gospel.

**HOMILY** – (1) Two women were out to lunch and began to discuss their marriage. One of the two ladies said, "we just celebrated our 50th anniversary." "That's a long time," the other said. The 50 year anniversary lady agreed, "a long, long time." Then she smiled. "You know what just occurred to me the other day?" she asked. "If I had killed him the first time I felt like it, I would be out of jail by now." (2) A wife and her husband were comparing which of them were the more intelligent. She said to him "I have a higher IQ, did better on my SATs and make more money than you," she pointed out. "Yeah, but when you step back and look at the big picture, I'm still ahead of you," he said. Surprised she asked, "How do you figure?" "I married better," he said with a smile. (Even if he wasn't as smart as she was, he was smart enough to know what to say!) (from *Laughter, the Best Medicine, Reader's Digest*, pg 163 & 175)

[at 4:00 Mass: I've been friends with the Woliver family for 35 years. I witnessed John's first marriage and buried his wife when she died and I had his second marriage to Theresa a year ago. I'm glad to be able to celebrate this occasion with them. At 10:00 Mass: I've been friends with Ralph and Jeanne for almost 40 years, and in the 40 years I've known them, I've known them to be very loving and dedicated spouses and parents. Their deep faith in each other and in God has always been an inspiration to me. I'm glad to be able to celebrate this occasion with them.]

As I read today's gospel about the widow, an idea related to our own day and age came to me. Widows in ancient times had very little social standing. They were, for the most part, dependent on their father or their eldest son for survival. Without a man to defend them, they easily became the victim of any kind of oppression. At least the woman in today's gospel had a voice with which she could defend herself. I am reminded of the 52 million unborn children killed in our country over the past 37 years since Roe v. Wade. They were entitled to life, liberty and the pursuit of happiness. Their DNA was the same as ours, but they only had our voice.

Now to the main point that our Lord teaches us about prayer. Our parable today is easy enough for anyone to understand. Often, though, we fail to understand why we must keep praying. We can easily understand how one person might eventually persuade another to give in to a request by their persistence; but why is it we need to keep asking God for something? Some people really believe God is too busy and so we need to get his attention, but he tells us God knows even how many hairs are on the top of our head, so we hardly need to get his attention. Some people think we need to inform him of what it is we need or want, but Jesus tells us God knows what we need even before we ask him. Some think they can wear God down like a child who continues to beg his mother for a candy bar he just has to have until she eventually gives in; some think perhaps God forgets, he is old you know; while some think they can get him to change his mind, as if he first thought something was a bad idea, but because he's tired of hearing from us he decides to give in to us. None of these ideas explain why we need to keep "bothering" him. Perhaps it is the opposite that is true, that he wants to hear from us more often. Perhaps it's we who are changed by prayer and not God. Perhaps we are the ones who forget he is our Father and by constantly going to him with our needs we grow in our faith in his love and wisdom. That may have something to do with Jesus' question at the end of the gospel: "when the Son of Man comes, will he find faith on earth?" There are all kinds of possible reasons why Jesus tells us not to give up when we pray, but for whatever reason we might conceive or might not we able to conceive, the bottom line is he tells us to not stop asking. All that's just been said is about only one form of prayer: the prayer of petition or supplication. Certainly we can't give up praying other forms of prayer too: prayers of adoration, love, thanksgiving and even contrition.

I would like to take a moment to speak of these other forms of prayer and not just the "asking for things" type of prayer. If we want to grow in our relationship with God, if we want to grow in knowing God, loving God, experiencing the peace and joy that only God can give, then we can't stop praying. In everyone's spiritual journey, there are desert periods, periods when we wonder if God is listening, periods when prayer gives us no consolation. All the saints have gone through periods like this and all of them say we have to keep on praying. To continue to pray during those dry times is to continue to grow deeper in faith, even in ways we are not aware of. Consistency in prayer, praying when we feel like it and when we don't is most important for our spiritual growth. This is one reason, among many, why we are supposed to come to Mass every Sunday, so we keep growing closer to God. That's what the Lord wants, and that's the mission of the Church to keep us growing in this way.

# 30th Sunday in Ordinary Time
## October 24, 2010

**HOMILY** – (Sirach 35:12-14, 16-18; 2 Timothy 4:6-8, 16-18; Luke 18:9-14) Today is Mission Sunday, a Sunday in October when there is a collection taken up all over the world for the missions. This collection helps support almost 200,000 schools, almost 18,000 health clinics and leprosy centers and over 1,000 dioceses. It's a very important collection for the worldwide Church. I will give you one hint of what they deal with. I have an Italian friend (my age), named Tony, who is helping to build a school for girls in Ethiopia. I had the opportunity to visit with him for a few hours recently when I was in Rome. One story impressed me. He told me when he went to Ethiopia many years ago, only about 10 % of the people wore shoes. Now it's up above 50 %. We suffer under bad times economically, but sometimes we forget how many people in the rest of the world are suffering to a much greater degree. There are special envelopes for the mission collection, but because this is a major collection, even if you put loose cash in the basket, it will go to the missions today.

This joke has been around for a long time. A young priest became the associate at a large suburban parish and after several months the pastor sat down with him to review his performance. The pastor said the young priest had been a true blessing for the parish, attendance was up, collections were up, the youth group was more active and a lot more people were coming to confession. The pastor complimented him even for the very creative way he designed a drive-through confessional. But the pastor said the assistant would have to get rid of the big sign in the front of the church that said, "Toot and tell or go to hell!" I've never heard of an actual drive-through confessional, but I don't think God would object. God is always ready to offer his grace to those who ask for his mercy and forgiveness.

We have two people in today's gospel who have come to the Temple to pray. The one thinks he will avoid hell because he's such a wonderful person; the other throws himself on God's mercy. The story would have shocked Jesus' listeners, because the Pharisees had such a reputation for holiness. They were a lay movement that had dedicated themselves to keeping God's law perfectly. Along with the 613 commandments of the Law, the Pharisees tithed, which was one of God's laws. As an additional practice, they fasted often. This particular one fasted twice a week, which was no small sacrifice. A tax collector, on the other hand, was included in the list of occupations considered "crafts of robbers," which no father encouraged his son to practice. Tax collectors were especially singled out, for the opportunity to cheat others was always there. Plus tax collectors usually were collecting taxes for the Romans – the Jews hated oppressors.

So, naturally Jesus' audience would have expected God to bless the Pharisee and pretty much ignore the tax collector. This parable, like all of Jesus' parables, had a surprise ending, an ending that forces us to think more deeply into God's ways, which are not our ways.

First of all, the Pharisee didn't have much of a prayer.

Jesus said, "he spoke this prayer to himself." He was pretty much saying, "thank you God that I am not a sinner like everyone else – even like this tax collector." He seemed to show no attachment toward God. His only attachment was to his own exalted image of himself. The tax collector, on the other hand, came to God for forgiveness and he received it. The key word here is "justified," which could also be translated "was made righteous." The tax collector went home justified; the other did not. The Pharisee's righteousness was of his own making; he didn't feel the need to ask God for anything. The tax collector's righteousness came as the answer to a prayer: "God, be merciful to me a sinner." It reminds us that holiness is God's gift to those who are open to his grace. All through the gospels, especially in Luke, Jesus is eager to offer his saving grace to anyone whose heart is open to it. This does not eliminate the need to live a holy life, to keep God's laws, to pray, to do good to others. The gospels certainly emphasize that, but the first step is to humble ourselves before the Lord and ask for his grace.

Archbishop Basil Hume, the Cardinal Archbishop of Westminster, spoke to a friend shortly before this death in 1999. He said, "If only I could start all over again, I would be a much better monk, a much better abbot, a much better bishop. But then I thought how much better if I can come before God when I die – not to say thank you that I was such a good monk, good abbot, good bishop, but rather, 'God be merciful to me a sinner.' For, if I come empty-handed, then I will be ready to receive God's gift." Not long after that the Cardinal died and the gospel of the Pharisee and the tax collector was read at his Mass. He knew how to bow low before God who blesses all those who come to him. (from *Celebration, Preaching Resources, 10/24/10, pg 2)*

As I reflected on today's gospel, I wondered if there was any hope for this Pharisee who tried to serve God with such fidelity all his life. Certainly! There is the hope that he would look deep into his own heart and realize how self-centered, pompous, judgmental and ungrateful he was in life. Maybe then he would do more than say thank you God that I'm better than everyone else. He would recognize that he is like everyone else, in need of God's saving love and grace for only Jesus is our Savior.

*Dear Friends, a few weeks ago I gave this homily. If you were here at Mass that day, you heard it. If you were not here, and there are reasons why some of our parishioners cannot be here on any given Sunday, I want to be sure you see it because it affects our very existence as a parish. I thank those of you who have increased your contributions since my appeal. I understand that many are doing all they can (it seems everything is going up except Social Security and pensions) and so I thank you for the sacrifices you make. If you did not hear this homily, please take a few minutes to read it. Fr. Joe.*

# 31st Sunday in Ordinary Time
## October 31, 2010

HOMILY – (Wisdom 11:22-12:2; 2 Thess. 1:11-2:2; Luke 19:1-10) A young couple were busy finishing their college programs and didn't have the time or money for anything other than church and going to school. One Sunday as they were attending Mass, the priest gave a sermon about marriage. "The three most common problems in marriage that can lead to divorce," he said, "involve money, children and sex." At that the young husband whispered audibly to his wife, "Then we should be okay. We don't have any of those!." (from *Laughter, the Best Medicine, Reader's Digest*, pg 290)

Well, today I need to talk about my least favorite topic: money. As important as it is, I do not mention it very often. I know all of you would get tired of hearing about it if I spoke about it all the time, and I would get tired of talking about it. But it's part of my job as pastor to keep you informed, so you don't find out at the last minute that we're in deep trouble financially. We're not in deep trouble, but you should know how things are going financially. I know all of you have a great love for St. Boniface or you wouldn't be here. I know that almost three-fourths of you drive past one or more parishes to come here and I am grateful that you do. Without your support and help, we would be history.

I try to limit my homily on finances to once a year and it has been about a year since I last approached the topic. I do send out letters about three times a year in order to thank people for their contributions, but those letters are primarily to say thanks and to let you know we are getting what you are giving.

Our fiscal year ends at the end of June. Two years ago we ended about $58,000 in the red. It was only the second time since I came here in 1991 that we ran over our budget. Last year we did better, we ran about $10,000 short. We had to take these losses out of our savings, which we were able to do, but we can't do that forever, and we can't print our own money to fill in the gaps. This past fiscal year we took a total of $147,000 out of savings. We had to take that much out in order to pay for the protective covering over our stained glass windows ($109,000), to make sure we could pay all other outstanding bills, and to give us a little cushion to begin this current fiscal year.

Where are we this year? We are behind; however, we hope to break even by the end of January. We are expecting to receive a bequest of $30,000 (the lawyers are still settling the will) and with that and a good Christmas collection (hint! hint!) we hope to catch up with our expenses. I might mention that bequests have been a great help to us through the years. It's a good way to continue helping your parish even when you have left this world behind. In addition to your donations, it is also thanks to those who went before us that we continue to enjoy this beautiful facility.

When I send out my letters three times a year, I am so very often impressed and am grateful for people's generosity. I have also noticed that among those who do not use envelopes, a lot more five, ten and twenty dollar bills are among the loose cash in the collection, which is a big help. I think many people are becoming aware that what a person could buy 20 years ago now costs significantly more. Compared with last year, so far our income has gone up a couple of thousand, but so have our expenses. I promised last year I would give back half my salary to help out and I have. I'm not bragging or complaining, just letting our people know I love St. Boniface too, and if I ask people to sacrifice, I'm willing to sacrifice also. By the way, I use direct deposit. It's so much more convenient than writing checks every week.

You're probably saying to yourself, lets get to the bottom line. What exactly am I asking for? Aware that it is a difficult time for everyone, I am going to ask for a modest amount: say a 5% increase if you can do it. I'll wager you will never miss it and I'll wager it will come back to you in some form or another. The Lord is not going to let any of us outdo him in generosity. I've always experienced that.

Our gospel today (Luke, 19:1-10) gives us some hint of our Lord's attitude toward wealth. Jesus did have wealthy friends – people who helped support him and the disciples. Here we meet a man, Zacchaeus, a wealthy man, who didn't have to give all he had to the poor, which Jesus asked of some of his followers, but who helped others with what he had as well as making amends for past sins of dishonesty. Jesus approved Zacchaeus' change of heart. The lesson for us in today's gospel, I think, is to remember what we have is a blessing from God, to use our resources wisely and prudently and to not be selfish. To those who unselfishly help our parish to keep doing God's ministry here in Northside, I say to all of you, "Thank you." Amen.

# All Saints
## November 1, 2007

**INTRODUCTION** – (Rev. 7:2-4, 9-14; 1 John 3:1-3; Mt. 5:1-12a) Our first reading is from the book of Revelation. The section just preceding today's passage describes the end of the world. The sun will become dark and the moon will become red as blood and there will be a great earthquake all over the earth. People will try to hide from all these terrible things and they will ask: "Who can survive?" Today's reading is the answer to that question – those will survive who have followed Christ faithfully. The number 144,000 is a symbolic number, symbolizing perfection. Notice after it refers to the 144,000 it speaks of those who are saved as such a large crowd that no one can count them.

**HOMILY** – It's hard to believe it's already November. As this year comes to an end we are reminded that time in this life will come to an end for each one of us. It's not something most of us enjoy thinking about, but the Church reminds us through various liturgies at this time of the year that this life is not all there is. God has greater things prepared for us. And so we begin the month with the feast of All Saints, giving us an image of the glory God intends for us if we just travel along the way he has pointed out for us.

The first reading today is from the last book of the bible giving us a lot of hope that we will be among those who will enjoy God's love for all eternity. Even though Jesus told us that those who take the easy way that leads to destruction are many, and there are few who enter into life through the narrow gate, those few are still quite a sizeable number, a number too large to count. Those who have been designated by the Church as saints are very easy to count. It's obvious that the great number of saints our first reading tells us about include ordinary people like us, or like neighbors we've known, or parents or grandparents or relatives we've loved. The hope that our first reading gives us is underscored in our second reading where we hear that "we are God's children." This is not just a nice, feel good, poetic term, it is in fact what we really are if we have God's grace in us.

Our gospel reading shows us Jesus preaching the beatitudes as he begins the Sermon on the Mount. As we hear the beatitudes, we can perhaps think of some of the great saints who lived out the various beatitudes. For example: "blessed are the single hearted" such as Mother Teresa, or "blessed are the poor in spirit" like St. Francis of Assisi, or "blessed are those persecuted for holiness sake" such as St. Lawrence or St. Boniface. Which of the beatitudes do you think appeals most to you? On this day of All Saints it might be a good idea to choose one of the beatitudes and try to live it out more fully. I believe if we do, we will find that we are at the same time living out all the others to a greater degree as well. "Let us remember that Jesus ends them with these words: "Be glad and rejoice, for your reward will be great in heaven."

# 32nd Sunday in Ordinary Time
## November 7, 2010

**INTRODUCTION** – (2 Maccabees 7:1-2, 9-14; 2 Thess. 2:16-3:5; Luke 20:27-38) Alexander the Great conquered every nation from Sicily and Egypt all the way to India. This area included Israel. He did it all in twelve years. In his spare time, when he wasn't busy conquering, he founded 70 cities. Alexander died at the age of 32 in 323 BC! At his death, his empire was divided among three of his generals. Our first reading today takes us about 150 years later to 175 BC when an ambitious Greek ruler named Antiochus IV came to power. He decided to unite his kingdom through religious unity. Thus it became a crime for the Jews to practice their Jewish religion. Circumcision was forbidden. Copies of the Scriptures were burned. Jews could not follow their dietary laws or celebrate their usual feasts. The worship of Greek gods and goddesses was required. Some of the Jews gave in to the Greeks, while others fought hard to hold on to their traditional faith. Our first reading gives us just a hint of how terrible this time was for the Jews who were faithful. If you look for this passage in your bible at home, it describes the torture of seven brothers and their heroic mother. A shorter portion of this reading was chosen today because it reflects the Jewish faith 175 years before Christ in the resurrection of all who are faithful to Yahweh. The passage prepares us also for the gospel, which deals with a question the Sadducees challenged Jesus with about the resurrection, something they did not believe in.

HOMILY – A man left his home in Chicago one cold November day to go to Cancun on vacation. His wife was supposed to meet him there a day later. When he got there he sent an email to his wife – only he mis-typed the email address. His email went to a recent widow who had just buried her husband. When she opened her emails she gasped and fainted. Her daughter, who happened to be home at the time, heard her fall and went to see what happened. She found this note on the computer screen, "My dearest, I just checked in. I can hardly wait to see you when you get here tomorrow. Your loving husband. P.S. It sure is hot down here." (from *Laughter, the Best Medicine, Reader's Digest*, pg 300) The Sadducees were an extreme conservative group among the Jews. They believed only the first five books of the Bible were the inspired word of God (not the prophets, psalms, historical books or wisdom literature). They did not believe in spirits, nor in angels. In spite of the general belief among the Jews that the dead would rise on the last day, as attested to in our first reading, the Sadducees did not believe in the resurrection. Someone humorously said that's how they got their name (Sad-you-see) because they didn't believe in the resurrection. The Sadducees represented the priestly aristocracy, so they were to be found mostly in Jerusalem, in the vicinity of the Temple. Jesus had, by this time, cleansed the Temple and driven the money-changers out, so it is possible that the cleansing of the Temple gave rise to this confrontation between Jesus and the Sadducees.

Since they didn't believe in the resurrection, they presented Jesus with a problem they thought would prove there could be no resurrection. They had a rule about a man marrying his brother's widow and producing children in his brother's name if the brother had died without children. This preserved the name and memory of the brother, it kept in the family whatever property the brother had, and it ensured that the widow would be provided for. Jesus answered the Sadducees by telling them they misunderstood marriage and they misunderstood the resurrection. Jesus is saying human language cannot describe the nature of the risen body when he says those who have risen will be like angels. In other words, resurrection will be nothing like the life we live now. Writers have tried to explain it and it seems to be best explained by what it is not: no pain, no suffering, no boredom, no death, no need for the things we now need to survive (food and rest) and no need to enter into marriages in order to keep our species from dying out. Probably the closest thing to heaven and the risen life that I can think of are those fleeting moments when we experience the love of another or the love of God. But it will be an experience that will be infinitely more profound than anything we now know and it will be forever. St. Paul, in Corinthians, compares the resurrection to a seed that grows into something wonderful and which no longer resembles the seed that had been planted. That is his way of explaining what is unexplainable.

At this time of the year, as nature begins to shut down for a few months, the Church is reminding us of the temporary nature of all things and of our own mortality. But in today's gospel it also reminds us of the hope we have, that God is not only the God of the living, but also the God who continues to create. Through his Son he is creating a new world, he is calling us to a new life. This new life is not just something we can expect to get automatically, which our present day culture tries to lead us to believe. It is a kingdom we are all invited into, but whether we enter depends on our free choice as to whether we follow the way Christ has shown us. Jesus has made that very clear: "I am the way" he told us. He is the unique Son of God, the very presence of God with us. Anything less is not the gospel, and assent to anything less will not make us disciples. It is not just an intellectual assent Jesus is asking of us; it involves being willing to hear Jesus' proclamation of God's will and doing it. (cf: *A Coming Christ in Advent*, Raymond E. Brown, pg 65 & 66). Amen.

# 33rd Sunday in Ordinary Time
## November 14, 2010

**INTRODUCTION** – (Malachi 3:19-20a; 2 Thess. 3: 7-12; Luke 21:5-19) In our first reading today we hear from the prophet Malachi who lived about 470 years before Christ. Many Jews at that time were apathetic about their religious duties and about keeping the Commandments. He warns his listeners that the day of reward and punishment is coming. Fire is the symbol that represents both the reward and the punishment. It will be scorching heat for those who have not followed God's ways and will bring warmth and healing to those who have been faithful.

**HOMILY** – An atheist was driving in the country when he came upon a priest and a rabbi standing on the shoulder of the road, fishing. Next to them was a big sign that read "Turn around. The end is near." The atheist took offense at the sign, so he rolled down the window and shouted: "Don't preach to me, you religious nuts!" A few seconds later the priest and rabbi heard tires screech, then a splash. The rabbi turned to the priest and said, "I told you we should've just written, 'Bridge Out Ahead.'" (from *Laughter, the Best Medicine, Reader's Digest*, pg 296)

A theme central to Jesus' teaching is the kingdom of God. For six centuries the Jews had suffered under one kingdom after another: the Babylonians, the Persians, the Greeks and the Romans. God had made many promises in the past assuring them that they were special to him and that they would be blessed in many ways because of his unique love. Even six hundred years of foreign rule did not dampen their hopes that God would liberate them from their enemies and from all their suffering.

When John the Baptist came on the scene, he told people to turn around (repent). The end is near. God would soon send his people a savior who would initiate God's kingdom. In preparation for this, John stressed the punishment that would be inflicted on sinners; Jesus, like John, proclaimed the kingdom was very near and sinners must change their ways. But, unlike John, Jesus put more stress on the joy of salvation. Jesus taught about the kingdom in parables; he cast out demons to show he was overthrowing the powers of evil; he healed people showing that indeed the kingdom was very soon to arrive.

As Jesus proclaimed the kingdom, a question that came up frequently was "when is this going to happen?" Jesus made it very clear that no one can predict when it would happen. Yet, in every age Christians have come up with predictions that pinpoint the exact time. Some of us might remember a recent book by Hal Lindsay: *The Late Great Planet Earth*. Every one of these predictions have one thing in common: they've all been mistaken. We hear in today's second reading that many of the Thessalonians expected Jesus to return almost immediately, so they gave up their jobs and sort of waited around for him. Paul told them to get back to work. If they didn't work, they should not eat; that is, they couldn't free load off the community. Jesus also said no one knows where it will be, for the kingdom is not a location that can be situated by longitude and latitude, but the kingdom of God will be obvious to all when it is established: "When the Son of Man comes it will be as evident as the lightening that flashes across the sky." (Luke 17:24) There is one thing Jesus did say most definitely, we must be prepared for it could come upon us very suddenly. Remember the parable of the man who went away for a while and put his servant in charge of the household. The master expected his servant to do a good job while he was gone. (Lk. 12:35-48) Being prepared means being ready to meet our maker at any time.

As much as Jesus proclaimed the joy of salvation, he was also a realist. Overcoming the powers of evil would be cataclysmic. Speaking as a prophet, we hear Jesus in today's gospel foretell the pains that would precede the birth of the kingdom. A discussion about the beautiful Temple leads into Jesus' prophetic words. The Temple would be destroyed and catastrophic events such as wars and natural disasters will come and go, but the end is not yet. First the disciples would suffer for being Jesus' disciples, just as Jesus would have to suffer. The powers of evil will not give up without a fight; the powers of evil will not frustrate God's plan of salvation. For those faithful to God, not a hair on their head would be destroyed.

Until Jesus comes again, we prepare for that day by gathering together in faith, by listening to his words, and by being nourished by his own body and blood. Sometimes life is a joy; sometimes it is a great struggle. In the process, God is making something new as the Book of Revelation tells us. In the end, for those who have been faithful to God, evil, sickness and death will not have its way with us; we shall rejoice in God's peace and love forever. Amen.

# Christ the King
## November 21, 2010

**INTRODUCTION** – (2 Samuel 5:1-3; Colossians 1:12-20; Luke 23:35-43) When the first king of Israel, King Saul, was killed in battle, the southern part of Israel (the tribes of Judah) chose David as their king. The northern part chose Ishbaal, King Saul's son, to be their king. Ishbaal was inept and after seven years of chaos, the northern tribes turned to David and asked him to rule them also. This is where our first reading comes in. David was a brilliant and far-sighted military and political leader. David was able to conquer his enemies on all sides. In spite of his serious moral misadventures, for which he repented, the Jews always hoped for another king with his talents and capabilities. Kings were anointed when they assumed office, thus the king was called "the anointed one." The Hebrew word for this is "Mashiah," or as we say it: "Messiah." As time went on, especially after the kingdom was destroyed by the Babylonians, the Jews longed for a king, a descendant of David, an anointed one, who would again rule in Israel and who would establish the peaceful and bountiful reign of God. When Mashiah is translated into Greek we have "Χριστός." So when we call Jesus "Christ" we are in effect saying Jesus, the anointed one; i.e., the King. Christ's kingdom is not an earthly one, as St. Paul tells us, but it is eternal and a sharing in God's own authority, power and glory.

**HOMILY** – After the evening meal, with father, mother and little five-year old Brian, mother left the family rather quickly. Brian wanted to know where his mother was going. Dad said, "Mommy is going to a Tupperware party." He thought for a moment, then asked, "What's a Tupperware party?" Dad always tended to give simple, honest answers so he said, "Well, Brian, a Tupperware party is where a bunch of ladies sit around and sell plastic bowls to each other." Brian nodded as if he understood, then burst out laughing and asked, "Come on, Dad, what is it really?" (from *Laughter, the Best Medicine, Reader's Digest*, pg71)

Brian could not picture a lot of ladies sitting around selling bowls to one another. The Jews, by and large, couldn't picture Jesus as their Messiah and King and they didn't think it was funny when the Apostles preached that he was. The Jews thought they knew what the Messiah was supposed to be: a glorious military and political leader, an idealized kind of King David who would overcome all their enemies, restore the kingship to Israel and initiate a reign of peace and prosperity. They also knew their Scriptures for they listened to them every week and they knew Deuteronomy 21:23 which said, "God's curse rests on him who hangs on a tree." They could not conceive of Jesus, a convicted criminal, crucified and hanging on a cross, as their Messiah. Pilate might have thought it some kind of a twisted joke that would embarrass the Jewish people to put a sign above Jesus' head, which said he was the King of the Jews. But, by and large, especially among the Jewish leaders, the idea of Jesus as Messiah was not only offensive, but blasphemous, and they were ready to punish anyone who acknowledged that Jesus was their Messiah, their king.

Jesus tried to tell them that his kingdom would be different from any kingdom they had ever known: "My kingdom is not of this world." Perhaps some of them could see how different his kingdom would be when they challenged him to save himself and he didn't. They knew of his amazing powers, but he chose not to use them to save himself. Instead he was willing to suffer extraordinary pain and humiliation to save us.

Think for a moment how great a faith the "good thief" had to be able to have to recognize Jesus as a king: "Jesus, remember me when you come into your kingdom." Nowhere in any of the literature of that time do we find anyone who anticipated their Messiah would have to suffer. Their Messiah would be a glorious, powerful figure. The "good thief" had to be able to see through all the expectations of the Jewish people; he had to be able to see through the weakness and failure that he was able to observe in Jesus and to affirm that Jesus was indeed a king. It is an act of faith that each of us must make individually if he is to be our king, and if we wish to be with him in his kingdom, a kingdom that will be for each of us the fullness of life that he came to bring us.

It is interesting that is was only 85 years ago that the Church established this feast of Our Lord, Jesus Christ the King. It was instituted as a corrective to the secular atmosphere of the times. However, as we can see in today's second reading. honoring Jesus as king has been part of the tradition of the Church from the beginning. This passage is "one of the most important theological statements about the person of Christ in the New Testament." (*The Collegeville Bible Commentary*, pg 1182) It proclaims that Christ existed before all creation and is preeminent among all creatures and that all things were created through his mediation. Therefore, he existed before all creation and is preeminent among all creatures. One verse is especially appropriate for this week of Thanksgiving as we read: "Let us give thanks to the Father, who has made you fit to share in the inheritance of the holy ones in light. He delivered us from the power of darkness and brought us into the kingdom of his beloved Son." "Let us give thanks," the letter to the Colossians says, it doesn't suggest we just say thanks. Giving thanks involves more than just saying it.

That brings us to why we are here today, to give thanks for God's many blessings, especially for bringing us into the kingdom of his beloved Son. Being part of his kingdom is an honor and a privilege that, although we do not appreciate it as much as we should now, we will praise God for all of eternity, and we will never grow tired of doing so. So let us give thanks to the Lord our God. Amen.

The 150-year anniversary of
St. Boniface Parish will be on
November 13, 2013.

# Glory, Glory, Glory Lord

by Rita Ring

VERSES 1,2,3

1. Glo - ry, Glo - ry, Glo - ry Lord! ___
2. Ho - ly Spir - it give___ us fire! ___
3. We are chil - dren of___ the Fa - ther.

You have ris - en from the tomb!
Fill us with___ Your ra - diant love!
He ___ has ___ a plan for us.

Give us (life Lord,) Your pre-cious life! You ___ have
Fill us with the fire of God's love! Mold ___ us
Come to Him as His lit - tle child. He who cre -

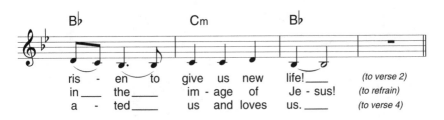

ris - en ___ to give us new life! ___ *(to verse 2)*
in ___ the ___ im - age of Je - sus! *(to refrain)*
a - ted ___ us and loves us. ___ *(to verse 4)*

VERSE 4

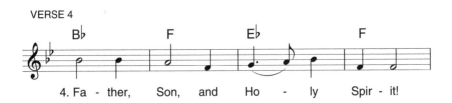

4. Fa - ther, Son, and Ho - ly Spir - it!

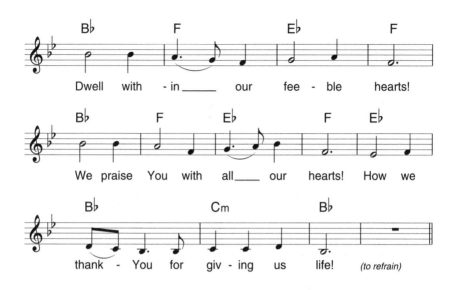

Dwell with - in ____ our fee - ble hearts!

We praise You with all ____ our hearts! How we

thank - You for giv - ing us life! *(to refrain)*

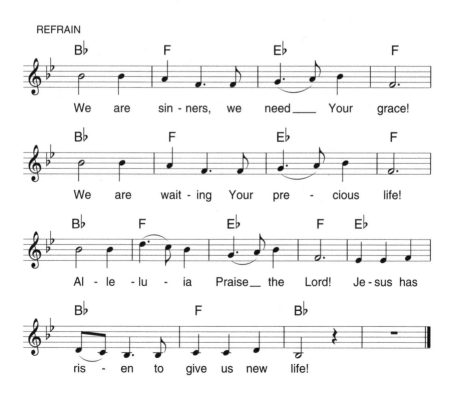

REFRAIN

We are sin - ners, we need ____ Your grace!

We are wait - ing Your pre - cious life!

Al - le - lu - ia Praise __ the Lord! Je - sus has

ris - en to give us new life!

# A Priest Is a Gift from God

by Rita Ring

**REFRAIN**

A priest is a gift from God. A priest is a gift from God.

This is My Bod - y, This is My Blood,

priest is a gift from God.

**VERSES 1, 3**

1. Come to Me, My chil - dren,
3. Come to Me, chil-dren of God,

I want to pos-sess your soul, I love you so ten - der - ly,
I want to pos-sess your soul, I give My-self to____ you

I want you to love Me too, A priest is a gift from God.
in the Ho - ly Eu-cha-rist, A priest is a gift from God.

I tell you My chil - dren, a priest is a gift from God. To -
I tell you My chil - dren, a priest is a gift from God. To -

day is the day the Lord has made, Wake, My chil-dren from your sleep,
day is the day the Lord has made, Wake, My chil-dren from your sleep,

## Prayer for Union with Jesus

Come to me, Lord, and possess my soul. Come into my heart and permeate my soul. Help me to sit in silence with You and let You work in my heart.

I am Yours to possess. I am Yours to use. I want to be selfless and only exist in You. Help me to spoon out all that is me and be an empty vessel ready to be filled by You. Help me to die to myself and live only for You. Use me as You will. Let me never draw my attention back to myself. I only want to operate as You do, dwelling within me.

I am Yours, Lord. I want to have my life in You. I want to do the will of the Father. Give me the strength to put aside the world and let You operate my very being. Help me to act as You desire. Strengthen me against the distractions of the devil to take me from Your work.

When I worry, I have taken my focus off of You and placed it on myself. Help me not to give in to the promptings of others to change what in my heart You are making very clear to me. I worship You, I adore You and I love You. Come and dwell in me now.

*Written by Rita Robinson Ring*

# Prayer Before the
# Holy Sacrifice of the Mass

Let me be a holy sacrifice and unite with God in the sacrament of His greatest love.

I want to be one in Him in this act of love, where He gives Himself to me and I give myself as a sacrifice to Him. Let me be a holy sacrifice as I become one with Him in this my act of greatest love to Him.

Let me unite with Him more, that I may more deeply love Him. May I help make reparation to His adorable Heart and the heart of His Mother, Mary. With greatest love, I offer myself to You and pray that You will accept my sacrifice of greatest love. I give myself to You and unite in Your gift of Yourself to me. Come and possess my soul.

Cleanse me, strengthen me, heal me. Dear Holy Spirit act in the heart of Mary to make me more and more like Jesus.

Father, I offer this my sacrifice, myself united to Jesus in the Holy Spirit to You. Help me to love God more deeply in this act of my greatest love.

Give me the grace to grow in my knowledge, love and service of You and for this to be my greatest participation in the Mass. Give me the greatest graces to love You so deeply in this Mass, You who are so worthy of my love.

*Written by Rita Robinson Ring*

# How to Become a
# Shepherd of Christ Associate

The Shepherds of Christ has prayer chapters all over the world praying for the priests, the Church and the world. These prayers that Father Carter compiled in the summer of 1994 began this worldwide network of prayer. Currently the prayers are in eight languages with the Church's *Imprimatur*. Fr. Carter had the approval of his Jesuit provincial for this movement, writing the Newsletter every 2  months for 6 1/2 years. After his death, and with his direction, we in the Shepherds of Christ circulated the *Priestly Newsletter Book II* to 95,000 priests with other writings. We have prayed daily for the priests, the Church, and the world since 1994. Associates are called to join prayer Chapters and help us circulate this newsletter centered on spreading devotion to the Sacred Heart and Immaculate Heart and helping to renew the Church through greater holiness. Please form a Prayer Chapter & order a Prayer Manual.

# Apostles of the Eucharistic Heart of Jesus

The Shepherds of Christ have people dedicated to spending two hours weekly before the Blessed Sacrament in the Tabernacle. They pray for the following intentions:

1) For the spread of the devotion to the Hearts of Jesus and Mary culminating in the reign of the Sacred Heart and the triumph of the Immaculate Heart.

2) For the Pope.

3) For all bishops of the world.

4) For all priests.

5) For all sisters and brothers in religious life.

6) For all members of the Shepherds of Christ Movement, and for the spread of this movement to the world.

7) For all members of the Catholic Church.

8) For all members of the human family.

9) For all souls in purgatory.

This movement, **Apostles of the Eucharistic Heart of Jesus**, was began with Fr. Carter. Please inquire. Shepherds of Christ Ministries P.O. Box 627, China, Indiana 47250 USA or 1-888-211-3041 or info@sofc.org

Father Carter requested
that these be prayed in Prayer
Chapters all over the world.

# Shepherds of Christ
# Prayers

are available in
Spanish, Italian, French,
Portuguese,and Polish.

Please begin a Prayer Chapter today.

# Shepherds of Christ Associates

## PRAYER MANUAL

Shepherds of Christ Publications
China, Indiana

Imprimi Potest: Rev. Bradley M. Schaeffer, S.J.
Provincial
Chicago Province, The Society of Jesus

Imprimatur: Most Rev. Carl K. Moeddel
Auxiliary Bishop
Archdiocese of Cincinnati

The Shepherds of Christ Associates Prayer Manual is published by
Shepherds of Christ Publications, an arm of Shepherds of Christ Ministries,
P.O. Box 627 China, Indiana 47250 USA.

Founder, Shepherds of Christ Ministries:
Father Edward J. Carter, S.J.

For more information contact:
Shepherds of Christ Associates
P.O. Box 627
China, Indiana 47250- USA
Tel. 812-273-8405
Toll Free: 1-888-211-3041
Fax 812-273-3182

# Chapter Meeting
# Prayer Format

The prayer format below should be followed at chapter meetings of *Shepherds of Christ Associates*. All prayers, not just those said specifically for priests, should include the intention of praying for all the needs of priests the world over.

1. **Hymns.** Hymns may be sung at any point of the prayer part of the meeting.

2. **Holy Spirit Prayer.** Come, Holy Spirit, almighty Sanctifier, God of love, who filled the Virgin Mary with grace, who wonderfully changed the hearts of the apostles, who endowed all Your martyrs with miraculous courage, come and sanctify us. Enlighten our minds, strengthen our wills, purify our consciences, rectify our judgment, set our hearts on fire, and preserve us from the misfortunes of resisting Your inspirations. Amen.

3. **The Rosary.**

4. **Salve Regina.** "Hail Holy Queen, Mother of mercy, our life, our sweetness, and our hope. To you do we cry, poor banished children of Eve. To you do we send up our sighs, our mourning, our weeping in this vale of tears. Turn, then, most gracious advocate, your eyes of mercy toward us and after this, our exile, show unto us the blessed fruit of your womb, Jesus, O clement, O loving, O sweet Virgin Mary. Amen."

5. **The Memorare.** "Remember, O most gracious Virgin Mary, that never was it known that anyone who fled to your protection, implored your help, or sought your intercession was left unaided. Inspired by this confidence, I fly unto you, O Virgin of virgins, my

Mother. To you I come, before you I stand, sinful and sorrowful. O Mother of the Word Incarnate, despise not my petitions, but, in your mercy, hear and answer me. Amen."

6. **Seven Hail Marys in honor of the Seven Sorrows of Mary.** Mary has promised very special graces to those who do this on a daily basis. Included in the promises of Our Lady for those who practice this devotion is her pledge to give special assistance at the hour of death, including the sight of her face. The seven sorrows are:

(1) The first sorrow: the prophecy of Simeon (Hail Mary).
(2) The second sorrow: the flight into Egypt (Hail Mary).
(3) The third sorrow: the loss of the Child Jesus in the temple (Hail Mary).
(4) The fourth sorrow: Jesus and Mary meet on the way to the cross (Hail Mary).
(5) The fifth sorrow: Jesus dies on the cross (Hail Mary).
(6) The sixth sorrow: Jesus is taken down from the cross and laid in Mary's arms (Hail Mary).
(7) The seventh sorrow: the burial of Jesus (Hail Mary).

7. **Litany of the Blessed Virgin Mary.**
   Lord, have mercy on us.
   *Christ, have mercy on us.*
   Lord, have mercy on us. Christ, hear us.
   *Christ, graciously hear us.*
   God, the Father of heaven, *have mercy on us.*
   God, the Son, Redeemer of the world,
   *have mercy on us.*
   God, the Holy Spirit, *have mercy on us.*

Holy Trinity, one God, *have mercy on us.*
Holy Mary, *pray for us* (repeat after each invocation).
Holy Mother of God,
Holy Virgin of virgins,
Mother of Christ,
Mother of the Church,
Mother of divine grace,
Mother most pure,
Mother most chaste,
Mother inviolate,
Mother undefiled,
Mother most amiable,
Mother most admirable,
Mother of good counsel,
Mother of our Creator,
Mother of our Savior,
Virgin most prudent,
Virgin most venerable,
Virgin most renowned,
Virgin most powerful,
Virgin most merciful,
Virgin most faithful,
Mirror of justice,
Seat of wisdom,
Cause of our joy,
Spiritual vessel,
Vessel of honor,
Singular vessel of devotion,
Mystical rose,
Tower of David,
Tower of ivory,
House of gold,
Ark of the Covenant,
Gate of heaven,

Morning star,
Health of the sick,
Refuge of sinners,
Comforter of the afflicted,
Help of Christians,
Queen of angels,
Queen of patriarchs,
Queen of prophets,
Queen of apostles,
Queen of martyrs,
Queen of confessors,
Queen of virgins,
Queen of all saints,
Queen conceived without original sin,
Queen assumed into heaven,
Queen of the most holy rosary,
Queen of families,
Queen of peace,
Lamb of God, who take away the sins of the world,
   spare us, O Lord.
Lamb of God, who take away the sins of the world,
   graciously hear us, O Lord.
Lamb of God, who take away the sins of the world,
   have mercy on us.
Pray for us, O holy Mother of God,
   that we may be made worthy of the promises of
   Christ.
Let us pray: Grant, we beseech You, O Lord God, that
we Your servants may enjoy perpetual health of mind and
body and, by the glorious intercession of the blessed
Mary, ever virgin, be delivered from present sorrow, and
obtain eternal joy. Through Christ our Lord. Amen.
   We fly to your patronage, O holy Mother of God.
Despise not our petitions in our necessities, but deliver us

always from all dangers, O glorious and blessed Virgin.
Amen.

8. **Prayer to St. Joseph.** St. Joseph, guardian of Jesus and chaste spouse of Mary, you passed your life in perfect fulfillment of duty. You supported the Holy Family of Nazareth with the work of your hands. Kindly protect those who trustingly turn to you. You know their aspirations, their hardships, their hopes; and they turn to you because they know you will understand and protect them. You too have known trial, labor, and weariness. But, even amid the worries of material life, your soul was filled with deep peace and sang out in true joy through intimacy with the Son of God entrusted to you, and with Mary, His tender Mother. Amen.

— *(Pope John XXIII)*

9. **Litany of the Sacred Heart, promises of the Sacred Heart.**
Lord, have mercy on us.
*Christ, have mercy on us.*
Lord, have mercy on us. Christ, hear us.
*Christ, graciously hear us.*
God the Father of heaven,
*have mercy on us* (repeat after each invocation).
God the Son, Redeemer of the world,
God the Holy Spirit,
Holy Trinity, one God,
Heart of Jesus, Son of the eternal Father,
Heart of Jesus, formed by the Holy Spirit in the womb of the Virgin Mother,
Heart of Jesus, substantially united to the Word of God,
Heart of Jesus, of infinite majesty,

Heart of Jesus, sacred temple of God,
Heart of Jesus, tabernacle of the Most High,
Heart of Jesus, house of God and gate of heaven,
Heart of Jesus, burning furnace of charity,
Heart of Jesus, abode of justice and love,
Heart of Jesus, full of goodness and love,
Heart of Jesus, abyss of all virtues,
Heart of Jesus, most worthy of all praise,
Heart of Jesus, king and center of all hearts,
Heart of Jesus, in whom are all the treasures of
    wisdom and knowledge,
Heart of Jesus, in whom dwells the fullness of
    divinity,
Heart of Jesus, in whom the Father is well pleased,
Heart of Jesus, of whose fullness we have all
    received,
Heart of Jesus, desire of the everlasting hills,
Heart of Jesus, patient and most merciful,
Heart of Jesus, enriching all who invoke You,
Heart of Jesus, fountain of life and holiness,
Heart of Jesus, propitiation for our sins,
Heart of Jesus, loaded down with opprobrium,
Heart of Jesus, bruised for our offenses,
Heart of Jesus, obedient even to death,
Heart of Jesus, pierced with a lance,
Heart of Jesus, source of all consolation,
Heart of Jesus, our life and reconciliation,
Heart of Jesus, victim of sin,
Heart of Jesus, salvation of those who hope in You,
Heart of Jesus, hope of those who die in You,
Heart of Jesus, delight of all the saints,
Lamb of God, Who take away the sins of the world,
    *spare us, O Lord.*
Lamb of God, Who take away the sins of the world,

*graciously hear us, O Lord.*
Lamb of God, Who take away the sins of the world,
   *have mercy on us.*
Jesus, meek and humble of heart,
   *make our hearts like unto Yours.*

Let us pray: O almighty and eternal God, look upon the Heart of Your dearly beloved Son and upon the praise and satisfaction He offers You in behalf of sinners and, being appeased, grant pardon to those who seek Your mercy, in the name of the same Jesus Christ, Your Son, Who lives and reigns with You, in the unity of the Holy Spirit, world without end. Amen.

**Promises of Our Lord to those devoted to His Sacred Heart** (these should be read by the prayer leader):

(1) I will give them all the graces necessary in their state of life.
(2) I will establish peace in their homes.
(3) I will comfort them in all their afflictions.
(4) I will be their refuge during life and above all in death.
(5) I will bestow a large blessing on all their undertakings.
(6) Sinners shall find in My Heart the source and the infinite ocean of mercy.
(7) Tepid souls shall grow fervent.
(8) Fervent souls shall quickly mount to high perfection.
(9) I will bless every place where a picture of My Heart shall be set up and honored.
(10) I will give to priests the gift of touching the most hardened hearts.
(11) Those who promote this devotion shall have their names written in My Heart, never to be blotted out.

(12) I promise you in the excessive mercy of My Heart that My all-powerful love will grant to all those who communicate on the first Friday in nine consecutive months the grace of final penitence; they shall not die in My disgrace nor without receiving their sacraments; My divine Heart shall be their safe refuge in this last moment.

10. **Prayer for Priests.** "Lord Jesus, Chief Shepherd of the Flock, we pray that in the great love and mercy of Your Sacred Heart You attend to all the needs of Your priest-shepherds throughout the world. We ask that You draw back to Your Heart all those priests who have seriously strayed from Your path, that You rekindle the desire for holiness in the hearts of those priests who have become lukewarm, and that You continue to give Your fervent priests the desire for the highest holiness. United with Your Heart and Mary's Heart, we ask that You take this petition to Your heavenly Father in the unity of the Holy Spirit. Amen."

11. **Prayer for all members of the Shepherds of Christ Associates.** "Dear Jesus, we ask Your special blessings on all members of Shepherds of Christ Associates. Continue to enlighten them regarding the very special privilege and responsibility you have given them as members of Your movement, Shepherds of Christ Associates. Draw them ever closer to Your Heart and to Your Mother's Heart. Allow them to more and more realize the great and special love of Your Hearts for each of them as unique individuals. Give them the grace to respond to Your love and Mary's love with an increased love of their own. As they dwell in Your Heart and Mary's Heart, abundantly care for all their needs and those of their loved ones. We make our

prayer through You to the Father, in the Holy Spirit, with Mary our Mother at our side. Amen."

12. **Prayer for the spiritual and financial success of the priestly newsletter.** "Father, we ask Your special blessings upon the priestly newsletter, Shepherds of Christ. We ask that You open the priest-readers to the graces You wish to give them through this chosen instrument of Your Son. We also ask that You provide for the financial needs of the newsletter and the Shepherds of Christ Associates. We make our prayer through Jesus, in the Holy Spirit, with Mary at our side. Amen."

13. **Prayer for all members of the human family.**
"Heavenly Father, we ask Your blessings on all Your children the world over. Attend to all their needs. We ask Your special assistance for all those marginalized people, all those who are so neglected and forgotten. United with our Mother Mary, we make this petition to You through Jesus and in the Holy Spirit. Amen."

14. **Prayer to St. Michael and our Guardian Angels:**
"St. Michael the Archangel, defend us in battle. Be our safeguard against the wickedness and snares of the devil. May God rebuke him, we humbly pray, and do thou, O prince of the heavenly hosts, by the power of God, cast into hell Satan and all the other evil spirits who prowl about the world seeking the ruin of souls. Amen."
"Angel of God, my guardian dear, to whom God's love commits me here, ever this day be at my side, to light and guard, to rule and guide. Amen."

15. **Pause for silent, personal prayer.** This should last at least five minutes.

16. **Act of consecration to the Sacred Heart of Jesus and the Immaculate Heart of Mary.**

"Lord Jesus, Chief Shepherd of the flock, I consecrate myself to Your most Sacred Heart. From Your pierced Heart the Church was born, the Church You have called me, as a member of Shepherds of Christ Associates, to serve in a most special way. You reveal Your Heart as a symbol of Your love in all its aspects, including Your most special love for me, whom You have chosen as Your companion in this most important work. Help me to always love You in return. Help me to give myself entirely to You. Help me always to pour out my life in love of God and neighbor! Heart of Jesus, I place my trust in You!

"Dear Blessed Virgin Mary, I consecrate myself to your maternal and Immaculate Heart, this Heart which is symbol of your life of love. You are the Mother of my Savior. You are also my Mother. You love me with a most special love as a member of Shepherds of Christ Associates, a movement created by your Son as a powerful instrument for the renewal of the Church and the world. In a return of love, I give myself entirely to your motherly love and protection. You followed Jesus perfectly. You are His first and perfect disciple. Teach me to imitate you in the putting on of Christ. Be my motherly intercessor so that, through your Immaculate Heart, I may be guided to an ever closer union with the pierced Heart of Jesus, Chief Shepherd of the flock."

17. **Daily Prayers.** All members should say the Holy Spirit prayer daily and make the act of consecration daily. They should also pray the rosary each day. They are encouraged to use the other above prayers as time allows.

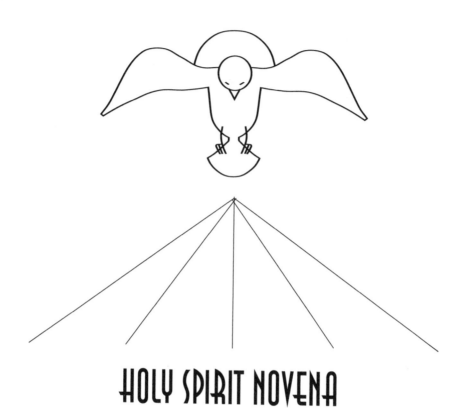

# HOLY SPIRIT NOVENA

**The Holy Spirit Novnea prayers are
also available in
Spanish, French, and Portuguese.**

**Shepherds of Christ Publications**
China, Indiana

This book is published by Shepherds of Christ Publications, a subsidiary of Shepherds of Christ Ministries, a tax exempt religious public charitable association organized to foster devotion to the Two Hearts, the Sacred Heart of Jesus and the Immaculate Heart of Mary.

For additional copies, contact us:
Shepherds of Christ Ministries
P.O. Box 627
China, Indiana 47250 USA

(toll free number) 1-888-211-3041
(phone) 1-812-273-8405
(fax) 1-812-273-3182
http://www.SofC.org

Nihil Obstat:
Rev. Daniel J. Mahan, S.T.L.
Censor Librorum
Archdiocese of Indianapolis

Imprimatur:
Archbishop Daniel M. Buechlein, O.S.B.
Archbishop of Indianapolis
Archdiocese of Indianapolis

First Printing: March, 1999
Second Printing: April, 2000

# DAILY NOVENA PRAYERS

## Opening Prayer

In the name of the Father and of the Son and of the Holy Spirit. Amen.

Dear Father, we come to You in the name of Jesus, in union with Him in the Holy Sacrifice of the Mass, in the Holy Spirit. We come to You united to the Child Jesus of Good Health and the Infant of Prague. We come to You in the perfect, sinless heart of Our Mother Mary, asking her powerful intercession, uniting ourselves to her holy tears. We come to You united to all the angels and saints, and the souls in purgatory.

## Prayer for Holy Spirit

We pray for an outpouring of the Holy Spirit on us, to be baptized by the Holy Spirit, that He will descend mightily on us as He did on the Apostles at Pentecost. That the Holy Spirit will transform us from fear to fearlessness and that He will give us courage to do all the Father is asking of us to help bring about the Reign of the Sacred Heart and the triumph of Mary's Immaculate Heart. We pray for the Holy Spirit to descend mightily on the Jesuits and the Poor Clares on the Shepherds of Christ leaders and members and on the whole Body of Christ and the world.

## Protection by the Blood of Jesus

We pray that the Blood of Jesus will be spread on us, everyone in our families, and the Shepherds of Christ Movement, that we will be able to move steadfastly ahead and be protected from the evil one.

## Healing

We pray for healing in body, mind, and soul and

generational healing in ourselves, in all members in our families, and in all members of the Shepherds of Christ Movement, the Jesuit Community, the Poor Clares, the Body of Christ, and the world.

## Prayer for Strength and Light

We adore You, oh Holy Spirit. Give us strength, give us light, console us. We give ourselves entirely to You. Oh Spirit of light and grace, we want to only do the will of the Father. Enlighten us that we may live always in the Father's will.

Eternal Spirit fill us with Your Divine Wisdom that we may comprehend more fully insight into Your Divine Mysteries.

Give us lights, Oh Holy Spirit that we may know God. Work within the heart, the spiritual womb of the Virgin Mary, to form us more and more into the image of Jesus.

## Prayer to Be One with God, Father, Son and Holy Spirit

We long for You, Oh Spirit of Light, we long to know God, we want to be one with Him, our Divine God. We want to be one with the Father, know Him as a Person most intimately. We want to know the beloved One, the Sacred Heart of Jesus, and live and dwell in Him at all times, every moment of our lives. We want to be one with You, Oh Spirit of Light, that You move in us in our every breath.

## Prayer to Be One in Jesus

Let us experience life in the Sacred Heart of Jesus, so we can say as Saint Paul, "I have been crucified with Christ and yet I am alive; yet it is no longer I, but Christ living in me...." Let us live, united to the Mass, all through the day being one in Him. Let us be able to love and know in this elevated state of oneness with our God. We long for Thee, oh beauteous God, we love You, we love You, we love You. We praise You, worship You, honor You, adore You, and thank You, our beloved God, Father, Son, and Holy Spirit.

## Prayer to Dwell in the Hearts of Jesus and Mary

We seek to be one in God, to live and dwell in the Hearts of Jesus and Mary, our little heaven on earth, to experience life in the all perfect, pure, sinless heart of our Mother. We want the Holy Spirit to move in us and to be united to Jesus as the Bridegroom of our souls and be a most perfect sacrifice offered to the Father at every moment as we unite in the Holy Sacrifice of the Mass around the world to help in the salvation of souls.

## Prayer for the Holy Spirit and His Gifts

Come Holy Spirit, come, come into our hearts, inflame all people with the fire of Your love.

*Leader:* Send forth Your Spirit and all will be reborn.

*All:* And You will renew the face of the earth.

We pray for the seven gifts of the Holy Spirit, we ask for perfection in our souls to make us holy, holy souls likened to God.

Dear Holy Spirit, we give ourselves to You soul and body. We ask You to give us the Spirit of Wisdom, Understanding, Counsel, Fortitude, Knowledge, Piety, and Fear of the Lord.

## Prayer for the Word Alive in Our Hearts

We know, dear Holy Spirit, the Word in His human nature was brought forth within the womb of the woman. We pray that His word will be brought forth in our hearts as He lives and dwells in us. We want the incarnation to go on in our lives. Dear Holy Spirit, work in us.

## Little Prayers to the Holy Spirit

Dear Holy Spirit, help us not to be ignorant or indifferent or weak, help us to be strong with the love of God.

Dear Holy Spirit, please pray for our needs for us.

Dear Holy Spirit, help us to respect God and to avoid sin. Help us to live in the Father's will.

Dear Holy Spirit, help us to keep Your commandments and to respect authority. Help us to love all things as You will us to love them. Help us to want to pray and always serve God with the greatest love. Help us to know the truth. Help us to have the gift of faith, hope, and love. Help us to know what is right and what is wrong.

## A Prayer for Intimacy with the Lamb, the Bridegroom of the Soul

Oh Lamb of God, Who take away the sins of the world, come and act on my soul most intimately. I surrender myself, as I ask for the grace to let go, to just be as I exist in You and You act most intimately on my soul. You are the Initiator. I am the soul waiting Your favors as You act in me. I love You. I adore You. I worship You. Come and possess my soul with Your Divine Grace, as I experience You most intimately.

# FIRST WEEK
# MEDITATIONS NINE DAYS

## 1. Romans 8:14-17

All who are guided by the Spirit of God are sons of God; for what you received was not the spirit of slavery to bring you back into fear; you received the Spirit of adoption, enabling us to cry out, 'Abba, Father!' The Spirit himself joins with our spirit to bear witness that we are children of God. And if we are children, then we are heirs, heirs of God and joint-heirs with Christ, provided that we share his suffering, so as to share his glory.

## 2. Romans 8:5-9

Those who are living by their natural inclinations have their minds on the things human nature desires; those who live in the Spirit have their minds on spiritual things. And human nature has nothing to look forward to but death, while the Spirit looks forward to life and peace, because the outlook of disordered human nature is opposed to God, since it does not submit to God's Law, and indeed it cannot, and those who live by their natural inclinations can never be pleasing to God. You, however, live not by your natural inclinations, but by the Spirit, since the Spirit of God has made a home in you. Indeed, anyone who does not have the Spirit of Christ does not belong to him.

## 3. 1 John 4:12-16

No one has ever seen God, but as long as we love one another God remains in us and his love comes to its perfection in us. This is the proof that we remain in him and he in us, that he has given us a share in his Spirit. We ourselves have seen and testify that the Father sent his Son as Saviour of the world. Anyone who acknowledges that Jesus is the Son of God, God remains in him and he in God. We have recognised for ourselves, and put our faith in, the love God has for us. God is love, and whoever remains in love remains in God and God in him.

### 4. 1 John 4:17-21

Love comes to its perfection in us when we can face the Day of Judgement fearlessly, because even in this world we have become as he is. In love there is no room for fear, but perfect love drives out fear, because fear implies punishment and no one who is afraid has come to perfection in love. Let us love, then, because he first loved us. Anyone who says 'I love God' and hates his brother, is a liar, since whoever does not love the brother whom he can see cannot love God whom he has not seen. Indeed this is the commandment we have received from him, that whoever loves God, must also love his brother.

### 5. 1 John 4:7-11

My dear friends, let us love one another, since love is from God and everyone who loves is a child of God and knows God. Whoever fails to love does not know God, because God is love. This is the revelation of God's love for us, that God sent his only Son into the world that we might have life through him. Love consists in this: it is not we who loved God, but God loved us and sent his Son to expiate our sins. My dear friends, if God loved us so much, we too should love one another.

### 6. Acts of the Apostles 1:1-5

In my earlier work, Theophilus, I dealt with everything Jesus had done and taught from the beginning until the day he gave his instructions to the apostles he had chosen through the Holy Spirit, and was taken up to heaven. He had shown himself alive to them after his Passion by many demonstrations: for forty days he had continued to appear to them and tell them about the kingdom of God. While at table with them, he had told them not to leave Jerusalem, but to wait there for what the Father had promised. 'It is', he had said, 'what you have heard me speak about: John baptised with water but, not many days from now, you are going to be baptised with the Holy Spirit.'

## 7. Acts of the Apostles 1:6-9

Now having met together, they asked him, 'Lord, has the time come for you to restore the kingdom to Israel?' He replied, 'It is not for you to know times or dates that the Father has decided by his own authority, but you will receive the power of the Holy Spirit which will come on you, and then you will be my witnesses not only in Jerusalem but throughout Judaea and Samaria, and indeed to earth's remotest end.'

As he said this he was lifted up while they looked on, and a cloud took him from their sight.

## 8. Acts of the Apostles 1:12-14

So from the Mount of Olives, as it is called, they went back to Jerusalem, a short distance away, no more than a Sabbath walk; and when they reached the city they went to the upper room where they were staying; there were Peter and John, James and Andrew, Philip and Thomas, Bartholomew and Matthew, James son of Alphaeus and Simon the Zealot, and Jude son of James. With one heart all these joined constantly in prayer, together with some women, including Mary the mother of Jesus, and with his brothers.

## 9. Acts of the Apostles 2:1-4

When Pentecost day came round, they had all met together, when suddenly there came from heaven a sound as of a violent wind which filled the entire house in which they were sitting; and there appeared to them tongues as of fire; these separated and came to rest on the head of each of them. They were all filled with the Holy Spirit and began to speak different languages as the Spirit gave them power to express themselves.

# SECOND WEEK
# MEDITATIONS NINE DAYS

### 1. John 14:21-31

Whoever holds to my commandments and keeps them is the one who loves me; and whoever loves me will be loved by my Father, and I shall love him and reveal myself to him.'

Judas—not Judas Iscariot—said to him, 'Lord, what has happened, that you intend to show yourself to us and not to the world?' Jesus replied:

'Anyone who loves me will keep my word, and my Father will love him, and we shall come to him and make a home in him. Anyone who does not love me does not keep my words. And the word that you hear is not my own: it is the word of the Father who sent me. I have said these things to you while still with you; but the Paraclete, the Holy Spirit, whom the Father will send in my name, will teach you everything and remind you of all I have said to you. Peace I bequeath to you, my own peace I give you, a peace which the world cannot give, this is my gift to you. Do not let your hearts be troubled or afraid. You heard me say: I am going away and shall return. If you loved me you would be glad that I am going to the Father, for the Father is greater than I. I have told you this now, before it happens, so that when it does happen you may believe.

'I shall not talk to you much longer, because the prince of this world is on his way. He has no power over me, but the world must recognise that I love the Father and that I act just as the Father commanded. Come now, let us go.

### 2. John 17:11-26

I am no longer in the world, but they are in the world, and I am coming to you. Holy Father, keep those you have given me true to your name, so that they may be one like us. While I was with them, I kept those you had given me true to your name. I have watched over them and not one is lost except one who was destined to be lost, and this was to fulfil the scriptures. But now I am coming to you and I say these things in the world to share my joy with them to the full. I passed your word on to them, and the world hated them, because they belong to the world no more than I belong to the world. I am not asking you to remove them from the world, but to protect them from the Evil One. They do not belong to the world any more than I belong to the world. Consecrate them in the truth; your word is truth. As you sent me into the world, I have sent them into the world, and for their sake I consecrate myself so that they too may be consecrated in truth. I pray not only for these but also for those who through their teaching will come to believe in me. May they all be one, just as, Father, you are in me and I am in you, so that they also may be in us, so that the world may believe it was you who sent me. I have given them the glory you gave to me, that they may be one as we are one. With me in them and you in me, may they be so perfected in unity that the world will recognise that it was you who sent me and that you have loved them as you have loved me.

Father, I want those you have given me to be with me where I am, so that they may always see my glory which you have given me because you loved me before the foundation of the world. Father, Upright One, the world has not known you, but I have known you, and these have known that you have sent me. I have made your name known to them and will continue to make it known, so that the love with which you loved me may be in them, and so that I may be in them.

## 3. 1 Corinthians 15:20-28

In fact, however, Christ has been raised from the dead, as the first-fruits of all who have fallen asleep.

As it was by one man that death came, so through one man has come the resurrection of the dead. Just as all die in Adam, so in Christ all will be brought to life; but all of them in their proper order: Christ the first-fruits, and next, at his coming, those who belong to him. After that will come the end, when he will hand over the kingdom to God the Father, having abolished every principality, every ruling force and power. For he is to be king until he has made his enemies his footstool, and the last of the enemies to be done away with is death, for he has put all things under his feet. But when it is said everything is subjected, this obviously cannot include the One who subjected everything to him. When everything has been subjected to him, then the Son himself will be subjected to the One who has subjected everything to him, so that God may be all in all.

## 4. Revelation 3:1-3,12,16-19

'Write to the angel of the church in Sardis and say, "Here is the message of the one who holds the seven spirits of God and the seven stars: I know about your behaviour: how you are reputed to be alive and yet are dead. Wake up; put some resolve into what little vigour you have left: it is dying fast. So far I have failed to notice anything in your behaviour that my God could possibly call perfect; remember how you first heard the message. Hold on to that. Repent! If you do not wake up, I shall come to you like a thief, and you will have no idea at what hour I shall come upon you.

Anyone who proves victorious I will make into a pillar in the sanctuary of my God, and it will stay there for ever; I will inscribe on it the name of my God and the name of the city of my God, the new Jerusalem which is coming down from my God in heaven, and my own new name as well.

'...but since you are neither hot nor cold, but only lukewarm, I will spit you out of my mouth. You say to yourself: I am rich, I have made a fortune and have everything I want, never realising that you are wretchedly and pitiably poor, and blind and naked too. I warn you, buy from me the gold that has been tested in the fire to make you truly rich, and white robes to clothe you and hide your shameful nakedness, and ointment to put on your eyes to enable you to see. I reprove and train those whom I love: so repent in real earnest.'

## 5. Revelation 5:9-14

They sang a new hymn: You are worthy to take the scroll and to break its seals, because you were sacrificed, and with your blood you bought people for God of every race, language, people and nation and made them a line of kings and priests for God, to rule the world.

In my vision, I heard the sound of an immense number of angels gathered round the throne and the living creatures and the elders; there were ten thousand times ten thousand of them and thousands upon thousands, loudly chanting:

Worthy is the Lamb that was sacrificed to receive power, riches, wisdom, strength, honour, glory and blessing. Then I heard all the living things in creation—everything that lives in heaven, and on earth, and under the earth, and in the sea, crying:

To the One seated on the throne and to the Lamb, be all praise, honour, glory and power, for ever and ever.

And the four living creatures said, 'Amen'; and the elders prostrated themselves to worship.

## 6. Revelation 7:14-17

I answered him, 'You can tell me, sir.' Then he said, 'These are the people who have been through the great trial; they have washed their robes white again in the blood of the Lamb. That is why they are standing in front of God's throne and serving him day and night in his sanctuary; and the One who sits on the throne will spread his tent over them. They will never hunger or thirst again; sun and scorching wind will never plague them, because the Lamb who is at the heart of the throne will be their shepherd and will guide them to springs of living water; and God will wipe away all tears from their eyes.'

## 7. Revelation 12:1-8

Now a great sign appeared in heaven: a woman, robed with the sun, standing on the moon, and on her head a crown of twelve stars. She was pregnant, and in labour, crying aloud in the pangs of childbirth. Then a second sign appeared in the sky: there was a huge red dragon with seven heads and ten horns, and each of the seven heads crowned with a coronet. Its tail swept a third of the stars from the sky and hurled them to the ground, and the dragon stopped in front of the woman as she was at the point of giving birth, so that it could eat the child as soon as it was born. The woman was delivered of a boy, the son who was to rule all the nations with an iron sceptre, and the child was taken straight up to God and to his throne, while the woman escaped into the desert, where God had prepared a place for her to be looked after for twelve hundred and sixty days.

And now war broke out in heaven, when Michael with his angels attacked the dragon. The dragon fought back with his angels, but they were defeated and driven out of heaven.

## 8. Revelation 14:1-7

Next in my vision I saw Mount Zion, and standing on it the Lamb who had with him a hundred and forty-four thousand people, all with his name and his Father's name written on their foreheads. I heard a sound coming out of heaven like the sound of the ocean or the roar of thunder; it was like the sound of harpists playing their harps. There before the throne they were singing a new hymn in the presence of the four living creatures and the elders, a hymn that could be learnt only by the hundred and forty-four thousand who had been redeemed from the world. These are the sons who have kept their virginity and not been defiled with women; they follow the Lamb wherever he goes; they, out of all people, have been redeemed to be the first-fruits for God and for the Lamb. No lie was found in their mouths and no fault can be found in them.

Then I saw another angel, flying high overhead, sent to announce the gospel of eternity to all who live on the earth, every nation, race, language and tribe. He was calling, 'Fear God and glorify him, because the time has come for him to sit in judgement; worship the maker of heaven and earth and sea and the springs of water.'

**Revelation 19: 7-8**
let us be glad and joyful and give glory to God, because this is the time for the marriage of the Lamb. His bride is ready, and she has been able to dress herself in dazzling white linen, because her linen is made of the good deeds of the saints.'

**9. Revelation 21:1-10**
Then I saw a new heaven and a new earth; the first heaven and the first earth had disappeared now, and there was no longer any sea. I saw the holy city, the new Jerusalem, coming down out of heaven from God, prepared as a bride dressed for her husband. Then I heard a loud voice call from the throne, 'Look, here God lives among human beings. He will make his home among them; they will be his people, and he will be their God, God-with-them. He will wipe away all tears from their eyes; there will be no more death, and no more mourning or sadness or pain. The world of the past has gone.'

Then the One sitting on the throne spoke. 'Look, I am making the whole of creation new. Write this, "What I am saying is trustworthy and will come true." ' Then he said to me, 'It has already happened. I am the Alpha and the Omega, the Beginning and the End. I will give water from the well of life free to anybody who is thirsty; anyone who proves victorious will inherit these things; and I will be his God and he will be my son. But the legacy for cowards, for those who break their word, or worship obscenities, for murderers and the sexually immoral, and for sorcerers, worshippers of false gods or any other sort of liars, is the second death in the burning lake of sulphur.'

One of the seven angels that had the seven bowls full of the seven final plagues came to speak to me and said, 'Come here and I will show you the bride that the Lamb has married.' In the spirit, he carried me to the top of a very high mountain, and showed me Jerusalem, the holy city, coming down out of heaven from God.

**Revelation 22:20**

The one who attests these things says: I am indeed coming soon.

Amen; come, Lord Jesus.

Scriptural quotations are taken from
The New Jerusalem Bible, Doubleday & Co.
*Imprimatur* granted by Cardinal Hume.

## Featured Selection: *Response in Christ* by Fr. Carter

The book, *Response in Christ,* comes at a very opportune time. In a thoughtful blend of the traditional and the modern, Fr. Carter gives to the modern Christian a message that will sustain him.

The most promising aspect of the book is Fr. Carter's gift about the Spiritual life. The Christian life essentially consists in God's loving self-communication to us with our response to Him in love. God gives us a sharing in His life in baptism. This life is nourished by the Eucharist. Father Carter offers reflections on how to deepen one's relationship with God: Father, Son and Holy Spirit. Item BN5 -$10

# Other great books published by Shepherds of Christ Publications

(To order call or write us at address in front of book)

**Shepherds of Christ Prayer Manual**
The Shepherds of Christ has prayer chapters all over the world praying for the priests, the Church and the world. These prayers that Father Carter compiled in the summer of 1994 began this worldwide network of prayer. Currently the prayers are in eight languages with the Church's *Imprimatur*. We have prayed daily for the priests, the Church, and the world since 1994. Associates are called to join prayer Chapters and help us circulate the newsletter centered on spreading devotion to the Sacred Heart and Immaculate Heart and helping to renew the Church through greater holiness. Please form a Prayer Chapter & order a Prayer Manual. Item P1 - $0.50

**Spirituality Handbook** Fr. Edward Carter, S.J. did 3 synopsis of the spiritual life. *The Spirituality Handbook, the Priestly Newsletter 2000 Issue 3* and the *Tell My People* book. The way of spiritual life proposed to the members of Shepherds of Christ Associates is centered in consecration to the Hearts of Jesus and Mary. All aspects of the spiritual life discussed below should be viewed as means to help members develop their lives in consecration to Christ, the Sacred Heart, and to Mary, the Immaculate Heart. Item P2 - $3

# Fr. Edward J. Carter S.J.

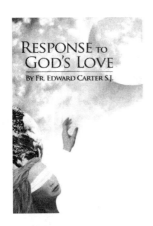

*Response to God's Love* by Fr. Edward J. Carter, S.J. In this book Fr. Carter speaks of God as the ultimate mystery. We can meditate on the interior life of the Trinity. Fr. Carter tells us about our uniqueness in the Father's Plan for us, how the individual Christian, the Church and the world are in the state of becoming. *Imprimatur.* Item BN4 -$10

*Shepherds of Christ - Selected Writings on Spirituality for all People* as Published in Shepherds of Christ Newsletter for Priests. Contains 12 issues of the newsletter from July/August 1994 to May/June 1996. Item BN1 - $15

*Shepherds of Christ - Volume 2* by Fr. Edward J. Carter, S.J. Contains issues 13-29 of the Priestly newsletter (September / October 1996 - Issue 5, 1999) Item BN2 - $15

# Fr. Edward J. Carter S.J.

**Shepherds of Christ - Volume 3** by Fr. Edward J. Carter, S.J. Contains Priestly Newsletter Issues 1 through 4 of 2000 including Fr. Carter's tremendous *Overview of the Spiritual Life*
Item BN3 - $10

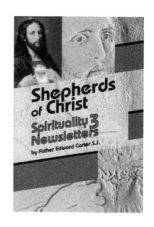

# Rita Ring

**Mass Book**, by Rita Ring. Many of the entries in the Priestly Newsletter Volume II from a spiritual journal came from this book. These entries are to help people to be more deeply united to God in the Mass. This book is available in English and Spanish with the Church's *Imprimatur*.
Item B8 - $12

**Rosary Meditations for Parents and Children**, by Rita Ring. Short Meditations for both parents and children to be used when praying the rosary. These meditations will help all to know the lives of Jesus and Mary alive in their Hearts. Available in both English and Spanish with the Church's *Imprimatur*.
Item B7 - $10

# Fr. Joe Robinson
### *(Rita Ring's Brother)*

***Guiding Light homily series - Steadfast to the Son - Cycle A*** — The sunflower is a great example of how we should be steadfastly guided by light. What a powerful thought that this exceptional plant is not stuck in one pose day in and day out, yet adaptable and magnetized to the sun. We feel the same about our Son. Our heads turns to face Christ as each day presents its challenges to find light. We join together like plants in a field and soak up the Son through the pulpit. We are a warm circle of strength using the wind of our breath to carry our priests' words, Christ's words, to new rich soil. Item C4 - $15

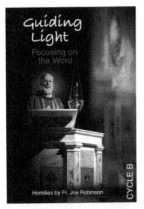

***Guiding Light - Focusing on the Word - Cycle B*** — At times we may feel that our path to Christ is a bit "out of focus". Like the disciples in the Book of Mark, this ordinary life clouds our vision of Christ's Divinity. We may doubt the practicality or possibility of applying His teachings and example to our modern life. Cycle B's homilies are a "guiding light" to help us realize Jesus' Messianic greatness and His promise of better things to come. Item C2 - $15

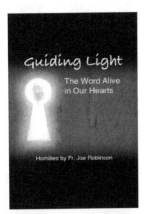

***Guiding Light - The Word Alive in Our Hearts. - Cycle A*** (partial) — Homilies by the Reverend Joe Robinson given at St. Boniface Church in Cincinnati, Ohio. It is a tremendous honor Fr. Joe has allowed us to share these great gifts with you – for greater holiness and knowing more and more about God. Item C1 - $5

# Fr. Joe Robinson

***Guiding Light - Feed My Soul - Cycle C***
— In a world rapidly advancing and encouraging personal gain, we are faced with modern problems. There is a challenge to find time in our busy schedules for Sunday Mass or a family meal. We are able to research, shop, bank and even work without hearing one human voice. It is no wonder that we may often feel disconnected and famished at our week's end. In Fr. Joe's third book of homilies from Cycle C, we are reminded of the charity that Christ intended us to show each other. We have a calling to turn the other cheek and be the Good Samaritan to others. We are rewarded with the Father's kingdom and love when we are not worthy. We are not left alone or hungry. Item C3 - $15

***Guiding Light - Reflect on the Word - Cycle B*** — The Word leaves an impression on our souls. In my thoughts and reflections are born a more tangible understanding of these eternal concepts presented in the Gospels and the readings. Anyone can read a sentence, but not anyone can absorb it's true meaning. Truth, in this day and age, is almost a matter of opinion or individual entitlement. We believe that Christ's truth is our Roman Catholic Church. We, as priests, champion it's teachings; we are ambassadors for the Pope and Christ to those faces looking at us. We are the light by which our congregation reads to reflect upon real truth and we do it hand in hand. Item C5 - $15

# Shepherds of Christ Ministries

*(You may copy this page to order.)*

<u>Send Order To:</u>
Shepherds of Christ Ministries
P.O. Box 627
China, Indiana 47250 USA

## *Order Form*

| | Qty | Total $ |
|---|---|---|
| BN5.  Response in Christ ($10) | ____ | _____ |
| P1.  Prayer Manuals ($0.50) | ____ | _____ |
| P2.  Spirituality Handbook ($3) | ____ | _____ |
| BN4.  Response to God's Love ($10) | ____ | _____ |
| BN1.  Shepherds of Christ - Volume 1 ($15) | ____ | _____ |
| BN2.  Shepherds of Christ - Volume 2 ($15) | ____ | _____ |
| BN3.  Shepherds of Christ - Volume 3 ($10) | ____ | _____ |
| | | |
| B8.  Mass Book ($12) | ____ | _____ |
| B7.  Rosary Meditations for Parents and Children ($10) | ____ | _____ |
| | | |
| C4. Guiding Light - Cycle A ($15) | ____ | _____ |
| C2. Focusing on the Word - Cycle B ($15) | ____ | _____ |
| C1. The Word Alive in Our Hearts ($5) | ____ | _____ |
| C3. Feed My Soul - Cycle C ($15) | ____ | _____ |
| C5. Reflect on the Word - Cycle B ($15) | ____ | _____ |
| Totals: | ____ | _____ |

Name: _____

Address: _____

City: _____ State: _____ Zip: _____

For More Information Call Toll free USA: 1-888-211-3041
or on the Internet: www.sofc.org

# A Song from Jesus

by Rita Ring

*Imprimatur:* Archdiocese of Indianapolis

# I Love You Jesus

by Rita Ring

**VERSES**

1. Oh Burn-ing Heart, Oh Love di - vine, how sweet You are to me. I see the host, I know You're here to love and care for me.
2. I can - not say. There are not words to say what my heart feels. I love You so, I scarce can breathe when You come in - to me.
3. Your ten - der Heart, Oh how it beats for love of each this day. I want to give You all my love, sur - ren - der to - tal - ly.

**REFRAIN**

I know Your love a lit - tle now, so dear You are to me. Come give me life, a - bun - dant life, I thirst to be with Thee.

*Imprimatur:* Archdiocese of Indianapolis

# Jesus is Life

Jesus tells us

### John 6:48-51

I am the bread of life.
Your fathers ate manna in the desert
and they are dead;
but this is the bread
  which comes down from heaven,
so that a person may eat it and not die.
I am the living bread
  which has come down from heaven.
Anyone who eats this bread
  will live for ever;
and the bread that I shall give
is my flesh, for the life of the world.'

### John 14:6
I am the Way; I am Truth and Life...

We live out His life, death and resurrection in our lives – Jesus is the bread of life. Jesus gives us Himself in the Eucharist. Jesus gives us His Word. We are living in the world with a purpose: God has created us and we are to die to those ways, not likened to Him and come forth living that life of resurrection in our lives. Baptism gives us a sharing in His life – In baptism our knowing and loving capacity is elevated. We have this capacity. We have been commanded in the greatest commandment to love God with all our hearts and love our neighbor as ourselves.

Fr. Carter says in *Response in Christ* "As we progress, we hope to show in detail that Christian holiness is <u>life</u> <u>in</u> <u>Christ</u>, for our life in Christ contains everything –

our love of God, our love of men, our love of all creation. We hope to portray the Christian as one who believes from the depths of his being that to live is Christ...

"Man rejected this self-communication of God in original sin. Yet God's desire to give Himself to man was not withdrawn. He determined to save man from his sinfulness, and thereafter the divine communication centered around the promised Redeemer."

Life is not life if it is not rooted in God.

Satan has pressed on man from the beginning in disobedience to a good God, a generous God, the Almighty and All Powerful and All Just. Satan wants this culture of death.

We live out the mystery of Christ in our lives. A constant dying to those ways not like Christ. Dying to vices and not giving into the deadly sins of seeking dominance for dominance sake, greed, pride, anger, envy, lust, jealousness, slothfulness. We rise to new life in Him – Our Christ-life – Our life in Jesus. Life in the Spirit. Life, Life, Life! Life is in Him.

This book, like *Response in Christ* tells us about life! Living in Christ – Dying to the selfish ways of the wounded human nature – God and His rules are first in our lives – We live to please our heavenly Father - to do His will – This is why we act – we operate in Him, our beloved God – We live in the Heart of Jesus - a Heart on fire for love of man.

The Father, Son and Holy Spirit dwell in our graced, baptized soul – We beg God to increase in us the virtues of faith, hope and love.

We go into the tomb at every Mass and die more and more to our selfish sinful ways to live more the life of resurrection in Him. In the Prayer before the Mass we pray with lavishing love to God – The greatest gift we can give to God is our obedience and love to Him.

## A Prayer before the
## Holy Sacrifice of the Mass

Let me be a holy sacrifice and unite with God in the sacrament of His greatest love.

I want to be one in Him in this act of love, where He gives Himself to me and I give myself as a sacrifice to Him. Let me be a holy sacrifice as I become one with Him in this my act of greatest love to Him.

Let me unite with Him more, that I may more deeply love Him. May I help make reparation to His adorable Heart and the heart of His Mother, Mary. With greatest love, I offer myself to You and pray that You will accept my sacrifice of greatest love. I give myself to You and unite in Your gift of Yourself to me. Come and possess my soul.

Cleanse me, strengthen me, heal me. Dear Holy Spirit act in the heart of Mary to make me more and more like Jesus.

Father, I offer this my sacrifice, myself united to Jesus in the Holy Spirit to You. Help me to love God more deeply in this act of my greatest love.

Give me the grace to grow in my knowledge, love and service of You and for this to be my greatest participation in the Mass. Give me the greatest graces to love You so deeply in this Mass, You who are so worthy of my love.

- *Mass Book*, December 27, 1995

At every Mass – we pray in the beginning to be forgiven for our venial sins, to be cleansed –

We receive the Bread of Life – We listen to the Word

– we are fed we eat His Body – we are fed – We are one in the Consecration – Praying to the Father united to the Holy Sacrifice of the Mass. We unite to Jesus in the Holy Spirit through the intercession of the Virgin Mary, with all the angels and saints and souls in purgatory, we pray.

We are one – begging for grace to be outpoured on this sinful world – We tell God we are so sorry for our sins and the sins of this world – I cry in my heart begging to God to hear My prayer –

I wrote the *Mass Book* for this – To tell the world about God and this intimate love union God wants with us – Come to me Lord and Possess my Soul.

## Prayer for Union with Jesus

Come to me, Lord, and possess my soul. Come into my heart and permeate my soul. Help me to sit in silence with You and let You work in my heart.

I am Yours to possess. I am Yours to use. I want to be selfless and only exist in You. Help me to spoon out all that is me and be an empty vessel ready to be filled by You. Help me to die to myself and live only for You. Use me as You will. Let me never draw my attention back to myself. I only want to operate as You do, dwelling within me.

I am Yours, Lord. I want to have my life in You. I want to do the will of the Father. Give me the strength to put aside the world and let You operate my very being. Help me to act as You desire. Strengthen me against the distractions of the devil to take me from Your work.

When I worry, I have taken my focus off of You and placed it on myself. Help me not to give in to the promptings of others to change what in my heart You are making very clear to me. I worship You, I adore You and I love You. Come and dwell in me now. — *God's Blue Book*, January 17, 1994

### A Prayer for Intimacy with the Lamb, the Bridegroom of the Soul

Oh Lamb of God, Who take away the sins of the world, come and act on my soul most intimately. I surrender myself, as I ask for the grace to let go, to just be as I exist in You and You act most intimately on my soul. You are the Initiator. I am the soul waiting Your favors as You act in me. I love You. I adore You. I worship You. Come and possess my soul with Your Divine Grace, as I experience You most intimately.

So in this culture of death — we know as members of the mystical body of Christ we are united to all the Masses going on around the world — The Mass the sacrifice of Calvary sacramentally made present — We say our Morning Offering — We give ourselves in total consecration to God — Our lives, all we do, united to the Mass.

---

SAY DAILY

GOD, I GIVE YOU MY LIFE IN UNION WITH THE MASS AS AN OFFERING FOR THE SOULS, THE CHURCH AND THE PRIESTS.

HELP US!

---

(this we use extensively, nursing homes etc.)

Here we have consecrations for children.

**Consecration to Jesus**

Dear Sacred Heart of Jesus, I love You so much and I give You my heart. Help me to love God. Help me to love my neighbor as a child of God. Help me to love myself as a child of God.

*Amen*

2009 © SHEPHERDS OF CHRIST PUBLICATIONS

**Consecration to Mary**

Dear Mary, my holy mother, I love you so much and I give you my heart. Help me to love God. Help me to love my neighbor as a child of God. Help me to love myself as a child of God.

*Amen*

2009 © SHEPHERDS OF CHRIST PUBLICATIONS

We are united ever deeper to each other as members

of the mystical body of Christ, by offering ourselves, united to the Mass in everything we do praying to the Father, in the Holy Spirit through the intercession of Mary our Mother with all the angels and saints and the souls in purgatory.

The Eucharist is the Mighty Medicine – God wants our love. **We need adoration chapels all over the world praying for these things.**

Fr. Carter, S.J. said Jesus gave him a message to have Apostles of the Eucharistic Heart of Jesus.

People spend at least 2 separate hours a week before the Blessed Sacrament praying for these intentions:

1. For the spread of the devotion to the Hearts of Jesus and Mary culminating in the reign of the Sacred Heart and the triumph of the Immaculate Heart.
2. For the Pope.
3. For all bishops of the world.
4. For all priests.
5. For all sisters and brothers in the religious life.
6. For all members of the Shepherds of Christ Movement, and for the spread of this movement to the world.
7. For all members of the Catholic Church.
8. For all members of the human family.
9. For all souls in purgatory.

Fr. Carter said Jesus told him on July 31, 1994 to pray these prayers in prayer chapters all over the world. We have them in 8 languages.

To combat the fear of death – we say the rosary and pray 53 Hail Marys saying – "pray for us now and at the hour of death"

Fr. Carter prayed the 7 sorrows after every rosary. He saw himself as a baby in Mary's arms – When he died he had a holy card of the baby Jesus in the arms of Mary clenched in his hand.

In the Shepherds of Christ prayers he put before the 7 sorrows – "Mary has promised very special graces to those who do this on a daily basis. Included in the promises of Our Lady for those who practice this devotion is her pledge to give special assistance at the hour of death, including the sight of her face."

Then in the prayers we pray the promises to St. Margaret Mary and we thank Jesus after every promise. The last promise says "I promise you in the excessive mercy of My Heart that My all-powerful love will grant to all those who communicate on the first Friday in nine consecutive months the grace of final penitence; they shall not die in My disgrace nor without receiving their sacraments; My divine Heart shall be their safe refuge in this last moment."

WOW! Jesus promises if we make the 9 First Fridays we will not die without receiving their sacraments; and His Divine Heart shall be our safe refuge in this moment.

Fear of death – God gives us so many gifts. What a gift this is - dying in the arms of Jesus and Mary – I am praying the Seven Sorrows every day – I knew of death, my mom and Fr. Joe's mom, died when I was 5 years old. Response in Christ – Living in Him. Going into the tomb and dying to our ways not likened to God.

Preparing ourselves for the beatific vision – Living deeply knowing God: Father, Son and Holy Spirit dwell in our graced baptized soul – Knowing God more and more deeply dwelling in us.

Jesus is truly present in the Blessed Sacrament in His Divinity and humanity – no less present than when He

walked the earth –

Come to me Lord and Possess my Soul –

The mission Fr. Carter wanted in the Priestly Newsletters was to get out the message that we go to the Heart of Mary, our spiritual womb and the Holy Spirit works to mold us more and more into the image and likeness of God. Here is a reflection from Fr. Carter.

# The Holy Spirit

**Reflection:** The Holy Spirit is given to us to fashion us ever more according to the likeness of Jesus. And the more we are like Jesus, the more Jesus leads us to the Father. Do we, each day, pray to the Holy Spirit to be more open to His transforming influence? Do we strive each day to grow in union with Mary? The greater our union with our Mother, the spouse of the Holy Spirit, the greater is the transforming action of the Holy Spirit within us.                    From *Tell My People*


Here is what Bishop Martinez says –

## The Holy Spirit and Mary

The late Archbishop Luis M. Martinez of Mexico strikingly speaks of the ongoing cooperation of Mary with the Holy Spirit regarding the reproduction of Jesus within us: "Christian life is the reproduction of Jesus in souls...

"Now, how will this mystical reproduction be brought about in souls? In the same way in which Jesus was brought into the world, for God gives a wonderful mark of unity to all His works. Divine acts have a wealth of variety because they are the work of omnipotence; nevertheless, a most perfect unity always shines forth from them because they are the fruit of wisdom; and this divine contrast of unity and variety stamps the works of God with sublime and unutterable beauty.

"In His miraculous birth, Jesus was the fruit of heaven and earth...The Holy Spirit conveyed the divine fruitfulness of the Father to Mary, and the virginal soil brought forth in an ineffable manner our most loving Savior, the divine Seed, as the prophets called Him...

"That is the way He is reproduced in souls. He is always the fruit of heaven and earth.

"Two artisans must concur in the work that is at once God's masterpiece and humanity's supreme product: the Holy Spirit and the most holy Virgin Mary. Two sanctifiers are necessary to souls, the Holy Spirit and the Virgin Mary, for they are the only ones who can reproduce Christ.

"Undoubtedly, the Holy Spirit and the Virgin Mary sanctify us in different ways. The first is the Sanctifier by essence; because He is God, who is infinite sanctity; because He is the personal Love that completes, so to speak, the sanctity of God, consummating His life and His unity, and it belongs to Him to communicate to souls the mystery of that sanctity. The Virgin Mary, for her part, is the co-operator, the indispensable instrument in and by God's design. From Mary's maternal relation to the human body of Christ is derived her relation to His Mystical Body which is being formed through all the centuries until the end of time, when it will be lifted up to the heavens, beautiful, splendid, complete, and glorious.

"These two, then, the Holy Spirit and Mary, are the indispensable artificers of Jesus, the indispensable sanctifiers of souls. Any saint in heaven can co-operate in the sanctification of a soul, but his co-operation is not necessary, not profound, not constant: while the co-operation of these two artisans of Jesus of whom we have just been speaking is so necessary that without it souls are not sanctified (and this by the actual design of Providence), and so intimate that it reaches to the very depths of our soul. For the Holy Spirit pours charity into our heart, makes a habitation of our soul, and directs our spiritual life by means of His gifts. The Virgin Mary has the efficacious influence of Mediatrix in the most profound and delicate operations of grace in our souls. And, finally, the action of the Holy Spirit and the co-operation of the most holy Virgin Mary are constant; without them, not one single character of Jesus would be traced on our souls, no virtue grow, no gift be developed, no grace increased, no bond of union with God be strengthened in the rich flowering of the spiritual life.

"Such is the place that the Holy Spirit and the Virgin

240 | Shepherds of Christ

Mary have in the order of sanctification. Therefore, Christian piety should put these two artisans of Christ in their true place, making devotion to them something necessary, profound, and constant."

*The Sanctifier*, op. cit. pp. 5-7.

So in summation – I see Fr. Carter when he did his doctorate on the Sacred Heart outlined much of what he said Jesus told him to do in the Shepherds of Christ in circulating over 17,000,000 Priestly Newsletters, loose and in books, to priests and hierarchy in these 18 years we have existed.

We circulated my brother's book of homilies – 5 times now – last year to the Pope and all the Cardinals in the world and all the priests and Bishops of the United States. (at least 40,000 of Fr. Joe's book last year to priests and hierarchy) His book is centered on the bread of life – on the Word and the Eucharist.

### John 11:25
I am the resurrection and the life.

Response in Christ

Praying the Shepherds of Christ Prayers in the tri-fold brochure, (available) for the priests, the Church and the world in 8 languages with the *Imprimatur*.

Mary said at Fatima until a sufficient number of people have consecrated their hearts to Jesus and Mary we won't have peace in the world. Mary said at Fatima: Bishops need to consecrate their dioceses to the Sacred Heart and Immaculate Heart - putting pictures of Jesus, the Sacred Heart and the Immaculate Heart of Mary, in their homes, businesses, Churches where Jesus is the King and Center of their hearts.

To have the vision of the heavenly Father for each one of us – each one of us uniquely created for a purpose to contribute to the Plan of the Father in salvation history – **We need adoration chapels around the world - praying for these things** –

1. For the spread of the devotion to the Hearts of Jesus and Mary culminating in the reign of the Sacred Heart and the triumph of the Immaculate Heart.
2. For the Pope.
3. For all bishops of the world.
4. For all priests.
5. For all sisters and brothers in the religious life.
6. For all members of the Shepherds of Christ Movement, and for the spread of this movement to the world.
7. For all members of the Catholic Church.
8. For all members of the human family.
9. For all souls in purgatory.

Please help us circulate these prayers and materials praying for the priests, the Church and the world.

Rita Ring, Co-founder
Shepherds of Christ Ministries

We pray for you from our Church in China,
24 hours a day before the exposed Eucharist.

We pray eight-day retreats for you every month.